The 39th Game:
Premier League plays at imperialism

Antony Melvin
Mark Carlton
Paul Grech
Colin Illingworth
Hugh Larkin
Paul Meadows
Stephen Orford

The 39th Game: Premier League plays at imperialism
ISBN: 978-0-9558570-0-3

Copyright © Antony Melvin, Mark Carlton, Paul Grech, Colin Illingworth, Hugh Larkin, Paul Meadows and Stephen Orford.

The authors assert their moral right to be identified as the authors of the work.

All rights reserved. No part of this publication may be reproduced, stored in a retrieval system, or transmitted, in any form, electronic, mechanical, photocopying, recording or otherwise, without the prior permission of the publishers. But I think we all know that if a website takes a fancy to any particular section they will rip it off mercilessly, without any credit, in order to earn a few pence from adsense.

The 39th Game: Premier League plays at imperialism

Contents

Chapter 1: 'Premier League mulls overseas games'................. 7
Chapter 2: Premier League 1992 – 2008 12
Chapter 3: The 39th step could be a good thing 28
Chapter 4: The 39th game would be a bad move................. 43
Chapter 5: 39th Game Has Logic... 57
Chapter 6: Eating at the top table 62
Chapter 7: Waiting On.. 85
Chapter 8: From European League To World League?........... 98
Chapter 9: What about the rest of us? 112
Chapter 10: The Greed League 125
Chapter 11: Premier League 2020..................................... 133
Chapter 12: 'Quotes'.. 147
Chapter 13: Was it worth it? 165
References 170

Acknowledgements

This book was written between February and April 2008 by a group of writers who, in addition to many other fine publications, write for what is left of http://www.squarefootball.net. During the book's development Squarefootball was one of thousands of sites hacked by the niha**** group and thousands of articles built up over a seven-year period were lost.

Back-ups are always a good idea in retrospect.

The book was edited by Antony Melvin; please be kind. And any errors left in are hopefully sub-libelous.

Anyway, the acknowledgements:

Antony Melvin: *"For Heather and George and their immense support that has given me the time to write and to all the fantastic writers at Squarefootball."*

Mark Carlton: *"For my Fiancee, Gemma, my Mum and Dad, Terry-Ann and John and my fantastic Grandparents, Eileen and Albert - you are all wonderful and thank-you so much for your support."*

Paul Grech: *"To Roseanne, My Wife"*

Colin Illingworth: *"I'd like to dedicate this book to my dad Robert "Wee Bert" Illingworth who sadly passed away during the making of this book. He was a true character and will be sadly missed but never forgotten. I'd also like to thank my mum for* *everything, my wife Claire for being so patient and understanding, Kenneth, Nigel and Beeby for their support and friendship and all of the fans that I have spoken to for the purpose of this book and for articles on the website."*

Hugh Larkin: *"For Jan and her patience"*

Paul Meadows: *"To Mum for sparking my passion for football and pointing me in the right direction; and for Toby, the best friend I've ever had."*

The 39th Game: Premier League plays at imperialism

The 39th Game: Premier League plays at imperialism

Chapter 1: 'Premier League mulls overseas games'

By Antony Melvin

"This is a huge strategic move, it's as big a strategic move that the League has made since it started, it makes the idea of putting a few games on pay-per-view nine years ago look relatively small compared with the idea of taking a whole round and playing it internationally."

Richard Scudamore. February 2008

The news broke slowly at first on the morning of 7 February 2008, with a Reuters report with a chillingly mundane title of 'Premier League mulls overseas games'.

Within minutes the implications were assessed and published. In the modern age of web reporting, news with truly global reach spreads faster than any known element. And sports news, especially about the world game, travels faster still. Einstein's ideas of space and time having a bendy quality would have been more easily understandable if he had known how quickly a 'Ronaldo to

Real Madrid' rumour could move. No doubt there are scientists currently being funded to falsify transfer rumours and then track how quickly they spread: to see if they are an accurate model for viral research.

The overwhelming consensus regarding the 39th game was instantly hostile, a money grubbing exercise that would destabilise the league and hawk the tattered remnants of football's soul to the highest bidder was a mild summation. Quite where many of the journalists found the time to peruse this moral high ground while considering Ashley Cole's nocturnal hobbies and Heather McCartney's mental health is another matter. But for once the fourth estate spoke with one voice.

Malcolm Clarke, chairman of the Football Supporters Federation, neatly summed up the initial hostility to the 39th game (or 39th Gam£ according to the Daily Mail). It was, he said:

"pure greed"

***

Richard Scudamore, the Premier League chief executive, had announced the 'international round' with seemingly no idea how badly it was going to be received. The initial plans were announced with gusto and not a little pride:

"This is a huge strategic move, it's as big a strategic move that the League has made since it started, it makes the idea of putting a few games on pay-per-view nine years ago look relatively small

compared with the idea of taking a whole round and playing it internationally."

Scudamore, however, was very quickly on the defensive; he was suddenly less popular than an Archbishop reading a book on Islamic crime and punishment. So the proposal changed shape; there was suddenly the option of seeding to keep apart the top five teams; fans would be consulted – some may even be flown out to watch the games. But the hostility remained overwhelming.

Suddenly, the chairmen and managers of the Premier League clubs were being asked to defend the plans; and to their credit they didn't hang Scudamore out to dry. Clearly, Scudamore would not have made the announcement without thorough backing from the clubs. And the clubs' spokesmen and owners quickly fell into line; David Gold was explaining his support on talkSport, David Gill on fivelive, Roy Keane in the press and so on. There were some dissenters like Harry Redknapp, but very few, initially, from within the professional ranks.

The lack of dissent from the professional ranks is hardly a surprise as football is hooked on money, and like most addicts the current dosage just isn't enough. Every season clubs look to bring in more money through TV revenue, ticket prices, sponsorship, scratch cards, lotteries, competitions, website subscription, merchandise, partnerships, stadium tours and so on.

And there is never an amount that is 'enough'; football clubs have become supermarkets where every two for one offer, every merchandised deal comes with the implicit understanding that you'll pay in other ways. The clubs even collude with the fans to say that season ticket price rises are needed to pay for players salary increases.

An example of just how much extra cash is now needed from fans only requires one to return to April 2000 when Manchester United wrote letters to season ticket holders basically telling them that the price increases for 2000/1 were needed to pay Roy Keane's wages:

> "... increasing the price at the lower end of the scale by £1 per match and others by £2 per match. Price increases are never popular but we are sure that supporters will recognise the importance that we place on staying competitive and being able to compete not only in the transfer market when appropriate, but in our endeavours to retain our existing players. In making this commitment (the earlier agreement of contract) to Roy (Keane), the directors believe they are also making a commitment to supporters."

The wage increase took Keane to £50,000 a week, seemingly necessary for one of the dominant players in English football. Football finances have since grown exponentially, and the extraordinary amount that Keane was awarded in 2000 is now commonplace for decent first-team players in the Premier League. Within five years of the fuss over Keane's remuneration Ashley Cole, the England left-back, was happy to publish his displeasure at an offer of £55,000:

The 39th Game: Premier League plays at imperialism

"When I heard Jonathan repeat the figure of £55,000, I nearly swerved off the road. 'He is taking the piss Jonathan!' I yelled down the phone. I was so incensed. I was trembling with anger. I couldn't believe what I'd heard."

To pay for the demands of footballers inevitably the fans have been asked to dig ever deeper. Season ticket prices regularly rise not by the previously objectionable £1 and £2 per match but by £5 or £10 a match for the bigger clubs; with the ever more business-like owners tentatively try to find the optimum balance between bums on seats and a ticket price that doesn't keep too many away. Owners want full stadiums because they sell more pies and programmes that way – and sponsors (or partners in the nuspeak) prefer to be associated with success.

Footballers want more and the club owners want a profit, in this environment is it any wonder that the Premier League started looking at alternative revenue streams?

And so the 39th game proposal has waxed and waned (but mainly waned), buffeted by a hostile press and a football community too far gone in its need for fresh financial fixes to abandon any new moneymaking opportunity.

But the essential questions remain: Do the fans want it? Can it work? Are there alternatives? How did we get here? Hopefully we can offer some clues.

Chapter 2: Premier League 1992 – 2008

By Mark Carlton

"Fifa cannot sit by and see greed rule the football world. Nor shall we."

Sepp Blatter

It is interesting that the addition of a further game to the Premier League calendar has been used as a high-profile example of what is symptomatically wrong with English football right now. The extra game to be played on foreign soil to promote extra revenue for the 20 Premier League clubs has many drawbacks, but if you can detach yourself from the situation and look at the prospect through corporate money-orientated glasses, rather than a passionate fan, there is an awful lot to celebrate about the Premier League business model.

In the most recent annual review of football finances in May 2007, Deloitte reported that Premier League clubs produced a combined turnover of £1.4 billion and contributed one quarter of the total revenue in European football, with this set to increase in the forthcoming years. With the Premier League being the dominant force in Europe, it is hardly a surprise that globalisation was on Chief Executive Richard Scudamore's agenda. Not satisfied with the £2.7 billion earned from television rights sold all over the world, which nets Premier League clubs on average £45million per season throughout the current television deal, the league seems intent on earning the clubs a further £5million from playing games all over the world.

These financial figures must have seemed like a pipedream over 16 years ago during the formative stages of the Premier League's conception. English football was at a low ebb, suffering from tragedy, hooliganism and a ban from European football for a combination of both these issues. Football grounds were not great places to be and something needed to be done to reignite the nation's interest in their game. In many ways the English game had stood still for far too long, whilst the European teams went from strength to strength. More revenue and the attraction of playing European football allowed clubs from Italy and Spain to build teams full of superstars, whilst the ban would leave English clubs years behind in development in an ever changing football environment.

England's World Cup campaign in 1990 started to reverse the damage and restore credibility to the nations battered pride. After a strong performance in Italy, the nations hunger for football was recaptured and with the lifting of the European ban, English football was allowed to rebuild its shattered image. Although Italia 90 did much to restore England's reputation, something drastic needed to be implemented to build on this great achievement. The game was still sadly lacking in funds to compete with the European elite. As early as 1988, plans were being made to revolutionize the way English football was to be structured in the future.

Money gained through selling television rights started to rapidly increase from a paltry £6.3million in 1986 for 14 live first division matches per season to £44million for 18 matches per season in 1988. By the time the Premier League was formed in 1992, that figure rocketed to £191.5million for 60 live matches per season, with BSkyB winning the rights for the next 5 seasons from the Premier League. With clubs sharing this magnificent bounty, football was yet again 'alive and kicking'.

We were promised a whole new ball game, when the Premier League began in 1992, coupled with Sky's glitz and razzmatazz, it certainly delivered. The initial breakaway from the football league was tentative, with 10 teams threatening to form a Super League so that they could capitalize on the influx of money into the game. The lure of more television money was eventually too strong with the number of teams threatening to leave the football league increasing to 16 in 1991. However, all 22 first division clubs eventually resigned from the league allowing the FA Premier League to be formed in September of that year.

***

With certain new concepts there normally follows vociferous debate about the pros and cons of the idea. The '39th game' is certainly the most radical proposal since the formation of the Premier League caused such furore itself. On the 15th August 1992 English football entered a brave new world as 9 matches were played on the first day of the season. With the benefit of hindsight, The Daily Telegraph accurately voiced concerns about the new Premier League format; little did they know that the traditional fixture list would be further decimated over the next few years:

> "At first glance, the nine match programme appeared to suggest that they had reverted to the original idea of an 18-club "Super League". But that was forgetting the needs of BSkyB and its satellite dishes, which look like becoming a major influence on the scheduling of fixtures..."

As well as a new structured top-flight, minor rule changes also gave the game a 'face-lift'. The introduction of the back-pass rule to reduce time-wasting by goalkeepers meant that we could consign the sight of shot-stoppers practicing their Harlem Globetrotters skills in the penalty area to the annals of football past.

The injection of television money started to filter through to the clubs with transfer fees soaring like never before. Newly promoted Blackburn Rovers led the spending with an English record transfer fee of £3.5million for Alan Shearer from Southampton; small change compared to the £15million fee that Newcastle United would eventually pay for him in the 1996-97 season. The millions spent throughout the first Premier League season, signalled the confidence of the 22 clubs as their finances initially improved with the dawn of the new era.

There is a degree of predictability about the Premier League these days, with the domination of the so called 'big 4', but in the

1992-93 season, things were very different. Manchester United established themselves as England's premier club after breaking a title drought that lasted 26 years. After taking 7 years to produce a team capable of winning the illustrious league title, Alex Ferguson finally found consistency with a blend of youth and experience, topped off with a dashing of flair in the shape of the Frenchman Eric Cantona.

United's challengers during the inaugural Premier League season did not consist of Arsenal, Chelsea or Liverpool, but Aston Villa, Norwich City and Blackburn Rovers. Norwich City led the table at Christmas only to fade away, with Aston Villa commanding the top spot for large periods of the season as well. Blackburn Rovers finished 4th, 13-points off the pace.

Liverpool, under the tutelage of Graeme Souness finished an uninspiring 6th in the Premier League, with Arsenal and Chelsea finishing even further from the summit in 10th and 11th respectively. The final Division 1 champions before the Premier League was formed finished just 2 points from the relegation zone. Leeds United struggled without the mercurial Cantona and failed to win an away game all season. Crystal Palace, Middlesbrough and Brian Clough's Nottingham Forest became the first teams to depart the Premier League being relegated to the new Division 1.

The 1993-94 season started with the first of three re-brandings in the Premier League's history. A sponsorship deal with Carling changed the competition's name to the FA Carling Premiership for the next 8 years.

The Premiership was now looking to build on a successful first season and establish the English league as one of the best in the world. However, English teams still languished behind their European counterparts when it came to the major European competitions. Arsenal went a long way to restoring English pride by winning the Cup-Winners Cup, beating Italian team Parma in the Final. Their victory in Copenhagen not only showed that English football was again on the rise and capable of competing with Europe's best, but also increased the amount of English teams allowed to enter European competitions from the next season. 6 English clubs would eventually qualify for European places in the 1994-95 season.

As per the majority of the Premier League's existence, Manchester United dominated the 1993-94 season, securing the double by beating Blackburn Rovers to the title and thrashing Chelsea 4-0 in the FA Cup Final. Manchester United narrowly missed out on the domestic treble by succumbing to Aston Villa in the League Cup final, losing 3-1. Blackburn Rovers continued to impress the footballing public by pushing United all the way in the title race building on a successful first season in the Premiership.

Rovers success showed that with heavy investment, football clubs could challenge for honours. Over the next few years clubs would try to emulate what Blackburn achieved, but more often than not throwing money at the situation ended in tears. With the influx of money coming into the game, not only domestically, but globally, the stakes were set much higher and success was imperative to keep up with the elite. Blackburn's gamble was to pay off in the following season, but their success had set a precedent in English football now, where wealth almost certainly determined league positions allowing the rich to get richer.

The 39th Game: Premier League plays at imperialism

***

After watching the England-less 1994 World Cup in the USA, the Premiership made a welcome return with the 1994-95 season being one of the best yet. The season returned with a new vigour, a new excitement as the league began to grow in stature.

This growth allowed the Premiership to attract some top stars to the game, leading to an influx of foreign players that has yet to cease. Some may say that this is a bad thing and has stunted any progress the national team has made. In 1994 though, it was looked upon as if the Premiership was achieving its goal, it was slowly becoming one of the most entertaining leagues in the world. Bringing big stars to the Premiership, such as German legend Jurgen Klinsmann who joined Tottenham Hotspur for £2million, helped to further increase the profile of the league.

With the season underway the league became more competitive. This would be the last season that the league would consist of 22 teams, with 4 teams suffering relegation to Division 1 meaning that the Premiership would be reduced to 20 teams from the following season. Teams unlucky enough to endure this fate included Crystal Palace, the perennial 'yo-yo club', Norwich City, Leicester City and Ipswich Town.

One of the closest battles for the title ensued with the resurgent Blackburn Rovers taking the title from Manchester United by 1 point. Jack Walker's millions delivered the league championship to the Lancashire club for the first time in 81 years after a frenetic final day. The finale to the league season was just the icing on top of a thrilling campaign which will be remembered for events such as Cantona's moment of kung-fu madness at Selhurst Park, George Graham's 9-year tenure at Arsenal coming to an end and the British transfer record being smashed 3 times in a year, with the moves of Chris Sutton (£5m), Andrew Cole (£7m) and finally Stan Collymore (£8.5m).

***

With the dust just about settling on the 1994-95 season, the foreign contingent began to increase further, with two of the biggest names in World football joining London clubs. Chelsea persuaded 32-year old Dutch legend Ruud Gullit to join the club from Sampdoria and Arsenal's new coach, Bruce Rioch, produced one of the greatest signings the Premiership has seen, bringing Dennis Bergkamp from Inter Milan for a fee of £7.5million. Newly promoted Middlesbrough also looked further afield for their playing staff by recruiting the exciting Brazilian Juninho. With the beginning of the season proving to be an exciting prospect, the Daily Telegraph reported that the English domestic game had a bright future ahead of it:

"The Premiership, financially strong and teeming with talent, both domestic and imported, has moved within sight of Italy's Serie A."

The 39th Game: Premier League plays at imperialism

With the Bosman ruling coming into effect in 1995 the movement of imported players would only increase as the limit on foreign players was abolished.

Although many clubs entered the transfer market with much gusto in an effort to catch the leading pack, Manchester United were still the dominant force, winning the double again in the 1995-96 season and retaining the league title the following season after pipping Newcastle United to the post for the 2nd year in a row. However, Manchester United were about to meet a new adversary in the shape of Frenchman Arsene Wenger. Wenger's introduction to the English game would spark a fierce rivalry between the two clubs and the coaches didn't necessarily see eye-to-eye either. Although the 1996-97 season belonged to United, a resurgent Arsenal side staked their claim to once again break United's title winning streak.

Arsenal successfully did that in the 1997-98 campaign, in Arsene Wenger's first full season at the helm. Towards the end of their title charge, Arsenal started to play football with a great style and panache that we now take for granted with Wenger's teams. A storming finish to the season meant that Arsenal won the Premiership by 1 point from United and going on to emulate Ferguson's recent achievement by winning the double, beating Newcastle United in the FA Cup Final. Wenger also became the first non-British/Irish manager to win the league title and was the only one until a certain Mr Mourinho came along a few years later.

The 1997-98 season signalled the beginning of the new television rights deal that was successfully retained by BSkyB after a huge bid of £670million was lodged for the next 4 years. This blew the previous deal worth £191.5million completely out of the water. The Premier League was truly becoming a sought after product.

***

As the Premiership headed towards the new millennium, Manchester United firmly placed England back on the map as a force to be reckoned with after winning the UEFA Champions League in dramatic fashion, as well as winning the Premiership and the FA Cup Final to cap a most astounding season for the club. Another tense final day meant that United snatched the title back from Arsenal and yet again underlined their domination of the English game since the Premier League began.

United's European win was something of a landmark for the Premier League. It had now achieved what it originally set out to do by making the league and its clubs a force to be reckoned with. English teams doing well in European competition was a good way to gauge how far the English game had come in the 8 years since the Premier League's inception.

Whilst there seemed to be a duopoly emerging in the Premiership, two other teams seemed to be making a push for the top; with Chelsea finding consistency for the first time in a many years and Leeds United finally rediscovering the form that won the title in 1992. This season saw the introduction of a third qualifying place for the Champions League, which was snapped up by Chelsea, but with that extra place being potentially lucrative, more clubs were spending haphazardly to secure that position.

The 39th Game: Premier League plays at imperialism

Leeds United were able to sustain their improvement in the 1999-2000 season, finishing 3rd and securing that Champions League Qualifying round place for the following season. Meanwhile, Manchester United won their 6th title in 8 years in extremely comfortable fashion and finished a massive 18 points ahead of Arsenal.

Another worrying trend appeared this season as Chelsea made history as the 1st team to field a completely foreign starting line-up, with not a single British player named in the 11. The influx of foreign talent had reached amazingly high levels and some pundits began to question whether this was having a detrimental effect on our game, including the potential negative outcome it may have on the national team.

For the third season in a row, Manchester United and Arsenal finished 1st and 2nd respectively as United stormed to the title again. Finishing 10 points ahead of the gunners demonstrated that clubs would need to do a lot better to catch Sir Alex Fergusons men. Leeds United continued to chase the dream by setting a British transfer fee record with the purchase of Rio Ferdinand from West Ham for £18million. However, their gamble didn't pay off as they finished outside the Champions League Qualifying spot by a point, leaving them with UEFA Cup football to look forward to after their brave semi-final exit in Europe's premier competition.

***

The Premier League received its 2nd re-branding as Barclaycard replaced Carling as the sponsor for the 2001-02 season in a deal worth £48million, however the league was now suffering from a degree of predictability, which has unfortunately plagued it ever since.

Arsenal broke United's three-year title streak to once again be crowned the best in England, but for the first time in Premiership history, United didn't finish in the top two, with Liverpool taking the 2nd spot. Leeds United again failed to capitalize on a large spending spree by failing to qualify for the Champions League, thus ending David O'Leary's tenure at the helm. Arsenal went on to complete Wenger's second double since joining them.

Normal service was resumed in the 2002-03 season, with United back to their resilient best. After trailing Arsenal by 8 points in March, they managed to overhaul this large deficit to win the league by 5 points. However the story of the season was the extreme fall from grace by Leeds United. By over stretching themselves in the quest for glory, Leeds were now paying the price for failure by not qualifying for the Champions League. What ensued was a mass departure of playing staff as the club drastically looked to recoup the millions they spent 'chasing the dream'. They avoided relegation by beating Arsenal in May in dramatic fashion and handing Manchester United the title at the same time.

The dramatic slide of Leeds United continued in the 2003-04 season, when they failed to avoid relegation at the 2nd time of asking. The plight of Leeds United was a welcome wake-up call for all 92 league clubs. Financial ruin was a very real prospect for any team chasing glory.

Whilst Leeds United battled to survive, Arsenal produced the most stunning display of consistency. Arsenal managed to be the first team since Preston North End in 1889 to go unbeaten through an entire league season; winning the championship by 11 points from 2nd placed Chelsea. The duopoly was becoming fragile when Manchester United finished 3rd as Chelsea's big cash injection changed the face of the Premiership forever.

Roman Abramovich had come to Chelsea's rescue in June 2003 when they were just days away from going into administration with debts of £80million. Abramovich's billions gave Chelsea a huge transfer budget to compete at the very top of the game. Some say that since Abramovich assumed control of Chelsea, the playing field has been skewed somewhat. Having access to almost unlimited funds increased the amount of money swimming around the transfer market, and as more clubs looked to compete on Chelsea's level, others have had to follow their lead and entice foreign investors.

Roman's roubles were not enough to beat an unstoppable Arsenal side this season – but it wouldn't be long now.

***

In 2004-05, the Premier League changed its name simply to the Barclays Premiership, and with a new sponsor came a new champion. The Premier League also successfully negotiated another increase in television revenue, as BSkyB paid £1.024 billion to secure the rights for the next three seasons. The league also brought in £320million by selling the international rights for three years as well.

With another large spending spree and a new manager installed in the form of Jose Mourinho, Chelsea won their first title in 50 years with the highest points tally in the Premiership's history. They managed to beat their nearest rivals, Arsenal, by 13 points achieving a total of 95 points for the campaign and after this season's performance, threatened to be the next powerhouse in English football. However, Malcolm Glazer may have had other ideas up his sleeve when he procured Manchester United in May 2005.

Although Chelsea won the title by quite a margin, the league season was one of the most exciting in sometime, especially at the bottom of the table. Sky Sports billed the final day of the season as 'Survival Sunday', where 4 teams battled it out with only one playing Premiership football next year. Eventually, West Bromwich Albion, the team adrift at the bottom of the league at Christmas managed to survive by beating Portsmouth and sending Southampton, Norwich City and Crystal Palace down.

Chelsea's dominance continued in the 2005-06 season as they retained the trophy by beating Manchester United by 8 points. Chelsea kept the other contenders for the championship at arms length all season, producing one of the dullest seasons since the Premier League began. Fans were also starting to vote with their feet. An overall decline in attendances of around 2% at the beginning of the season demonstrated that some fans would no longer pay exorbitant ticket prices and were fed up with the ever erratic fixture scheduling to suit the television companies. Small chinks in the Premier League's armour were beginning to show.

The 39th Game: Premier League plays at imperialism

***

Manchester United finally regained the Premier League trophy in the 2006-07 season after a 3 year absence, with Chelsea 6 points behind in 2nd. This would be a season remembered for the dramatic increase in foreign owners, as Liverpool, Aston Villa and West Ham all followed Chelsea and Manchester United's blueprint.

United then repeated their success in 2007/8, but in a much tighter contest. With two games left Chelsea, Manchester United or Arsenal could have been champions; and Chelsea and United went into the final game ahead of Chelsea on goal difference with Arsenal four points back. United won the last game of the season to edge out Chelsea and also beat Chelsea in the Champions' League final – confirmation that the Premier League was now the strongest league in Europe.

***

The Premier League had truly become a global entity now, with the league securing £625million from international television rights, almost double the previous deal. Richard Scudamore certainly knows that the Premier League is a product that produces cash, and lots of it.

Scudamore sees 'the 39th game' as the next logical step towards global sporting domination and we can't argue that progressive thinking is better than standing still and playing catch-up, we just have to take one look at the Premier League's illustrious history to prove that point. However, Scudamore's progressive thinking may be better suited to other ideas, such as trying to develop a level playing field for the 20 Premier League teams perhaps? Is the 39th game truly the right way for the Premier League to develop?

Chapter 3: The 39th step could be a good thing

By Antony Melvin

> *"I go to the finest stadia ever and watch some of the quickest, slickest, most exciting football. Everybody is coming at us. The Premier League is so pervasive, so much part of news, front and back of papers, that basically all the world wants a big slice of us."*

Richard Scudamore, September 2007

The knee-jerk reaction to Richard Scudamore's announcement of an 'international round' was always going to be negative. There are some suggestions that the Premier League takes too much stock of the opinion of loud-mouthed Islington types (or Hoxton or or Shoreditch or wherever the place to be seen to be living in the capital is this week); Scudamore's almost bemused responses to the initial hostility to his plan probably confirm this.

But is the concept of football clubs looking to generate more money fundamentally evil?

***

The 39th Game: Premier League plays at imperialism

There has been any number of pundits displaying their moral credentials for saying that this is a stupid, moneymaking exercise; as if that in itself is wrong. And of course this is an exercise in generating money, however anyone wants to dress it up. Arsene Wenger can describe it as taking the game to the:

"90 per cent [of our fans who] have no access at all to competitive games"

... but a more accurate description would be to explore the opportunity to take a few quid from the 90% of fans outside of England. But if we can cut through all the guff about morality and just accept it as a way to make money why is that so bad?

Sports organisations have to generate money, whether through sponsorship, TV exposure, ticket sales, rich benefactors or whatever. The arguments against raising money are predicated on morality; so is the 39th step a good thing? Or perhaps in these amoral times it is only necessary for the 39th step not to be too much of a bad thing.

Is it the case that somehow all the other moneymaking schemes that the Premier League and its individual clubs have come up are OK and this one is not? For my money allowing the TV companies to destroy the 3pm Saturday kick-off was a bad thing, but that was not widely condemned; I don't remember John Major or Neil Kinnock suggesting that supporters should be protected from the evil of Monday night kick-offs.

Is selling the name of a club's ground to the highest bidder better than an international round?

Is handing FA Cup final tickets to disinterested corporate clones at the expense of real fans a more moral position?

Are bond schemes that force fans to pay a lump sum to allow them the privilege of handing over another lump each season to attend matches fair?

Is the enforced purchase of unwanted cup tickets somehow reasonable?

Of course not but all of these ideas have been proposed or implemented at various times, but none received such a vitriolic press greeting as the 39th game proposal.

English football at the top level crossed its own Rubicon in 1992 when the Premier League was formed; it has already sold its populist soul and has encouraged every and any initiative that could enrich the richest clubs in England. To suggest that an international round is immoral is to deny history.

The advantage enjoyed by the biggest clubs is now so immense that it will take something fairly innovative to give the also-rans hope in the long-term. It could be that the 39th game is that innovation.

***

The 39th game may have been born as an idea steeped in avarice, but it could yet be a way to help redistribute wealth and create a more competitive, more traditional fixture list.

To understand English football you have to understand that its roots lie in the pyramid and in dreams. The ability that any team from any geographical place in England (although probably no longer Wales) backed by whatever motley collection of local retailers and grandees can, potentially, be promoted to the elite is part of the dream. That such a club can go on to win the title is, unfortunately, merely a fairytale.

There is almost no hope that any team that can climb through the divisions from non-league football can make any impact in the top flight without a stack of cash; look at Wimbledon who successfully moved through the divisions into the top flight in barely 10 years, before collapsing into a franchised MK Dons and a fans owned AFC Wimbledon side. Wigan Athletic continues to cling to their status in the top-flight, but gravity will inevitably grasp them, whether this season or not.

The harsh reality is that only 23 different teams have ever topped English football at the end of any of its 108 seasons; and if you reduce that to the 61 seasons since football resumed in 1947 the champion teams number just 15. If there were 15 teams in with a shot at the title then everyone would be excited. Sadly the formation of the Premier League in 1992 exacerbated the measures introduced earlier like home teams not having to share the attendance money – which destroyed the very fabric of the competition with barely a voice raised against it – and has meant that the title is now a rich clubs' plaything.

When Liverpool dominated the division from 1973 to 1990 it was only partly as a result of the moneyed teams of Manchester and London hitting fallow patches. Leeds, Derby, Nottingham Forest, Aston Villa, Everton and a rising Arsenal all won the title in those years as well as Liverpool suggesting that a good manager could assemble a squad at almost any reasonably well supported and financed club and make a run for the title.

When the Premier League came along in 1992 it offered a way to bail out debt-ridden clubs in crumbling stadiums under siege from meddling politicians and rampant hooliganism. But the cost of those shiny, plastic seats has been a sterilisation of both the atmosphere and the competition. The 39th game can hardly worsen the title hopes of the teams outside the 'big four' – can it?

***

A well run club with a good manager can no longer hope to be champions; now the best a well-run club can hope for is a mid-table finish or even the Pyrrhic victory of a UEFA Cup spot – usually as long as they have divested themselves of the distractions of the domestic cups quickly enough.

Since the Premier League arrived there have been just four winners in sixteen seasons. Only Blackburn Rovers funded by a multi-millionaire benefactor has been able to break the financial stranglehold of the three richest clubs in their 1995 title success.

This is the real problem with the Premier League, not that teams can't get into it or even stay in it. It is that only three very rich clubs can win it; that is until Liverpool stop trying to fight this new order with the wrong weapons. In the past players were impressed by history and tradition – now they just want the money.

The idea that there is too big a gap between the Premier League and the Championship (divisions one and two in old money) has been proved to be a nonsense in recent years. Promoted team after promoted team has defied the bookmakers who always post them as odds-on to return to the financial underworld of the football league. The fact is that the majority of promoted sides are not relegated immediately, and since 1992, 40 different sides have competed in the top flight of English football.

Of these 40 sides only seven have remained in the Premier League for each of its 16 years; the perennial champions of Arsenal, Chelsea and Manchester United plus the English football's most successful team, Liverpool, and the deep-rooted challenge of Everton, Tottenham Hotspur and Aston Villa. By remaining in the Premier League for its duration these seven have acquired so much cash that it almost guarantees success.

The top six of the Premier League, in 2007/8, were (in order):
1. Manchester United
2. Chelsea
3. Arsenal
4. Liverpool
5. Everton
6. Aston Villa

Tottenham finished 11th, and beat Chelsea in the League Cup Final. The teams that stay in the top flight for any length of time hoover up so much cash that eventually they are bound to employ a coach or manager with enough acumen to turn it into silverware. The Premier League alchemists are capable of turning gold into silver.

Many of the critics of the 39th game suggest that an international round will entrench advantage. This is naively similar to the lampooning that a 2007 Conservative press briefing got on

'Have I Got News For You'. The Conservative Party produced a report looking to abolish Grammar schools because they 'entrench advantage'; when the reality is that many Conservative voters like grammar schools, simply because they 'entrench advantage'.

The teams with the most money win the league under the current system. It is largely irrelevant how this money is generated or spent; some teams like to commit more money to youth development and some to big-name transfers. But regardless of how fans like to play around with comparing transfer fees like they were Panini stickers – look you've got eight players who cost more than £10m and we've only got six – the biggest clubs always win under the current system.

***

The only way to break this cycle is to generate revenue for clubs that is more evenly distributed.

What is true is that although the bottom half of the table remains a democracy, where clubs can join for a while when they have navigated the lottery of the Championship, the top half of the top half is an oligopoly. There is little chance of any team breaking into the top four or five without spending an awful lot of cash, unless they happen to have an exceptional manager with a patient owner and an understanding set of fans. Martin O'Neill at Aston Villa and David Moyes at Everton immediately spring to mind as two of the few set-ups that could manage to bridge the gap; Rafa Benitez at Liverpool has two of these three traits (as the owners remain a worry) and Juande Ramos at Spurs perhaps two and a half.

So although the top three keep dominating the title race there is hope that four more teams have the financial clout to bridge the gap; and let's be clear on that fact. Finances are required to allow teams to compete – having a great manager and a tremendous support is not enough in itself.

The Premier League is awash with money, the average club has never been so rich – nine of the richest 20 clubs in Europe are English; and European clubs are the most profitable in the world. So why can only three teams get within a sociable distance of the title?

Simply put the Premier League has entrenched advantage since it was formed and the end result is a league that is so lopsided that unless something ingenious happens the next decade could see the same three teams (plus almost certainly Liverpool) win every single title. Is this good for anyone?

If the first 25 Premier League seasons see every title shared between the same three teams (excluding the increasingly anomalous Blackburn Rovers win) will English football be the winner?

***

I'm not convinced that the 39th step is ingenious enough to solve all the woes that entrenched advantage has brought, but it is a chance to redistribute some of the wealth in the top flight. And without something innovative like the 39th game there may never be a way to help level the financial imbalance in the top-flight. How are the likes of Aston Villa and Tottenham Hotspur ever going to compete for the title in the current set-up with the advantage so entrenched with a handful of teams?

A 39th game would bring the also-rans of the Premier League into the consciousness of foreign fans and enable them to start to erode the natural advantage that the well established teams enjoy. It may seem laughable now to suggest that Wigan could generate a huge international fanbase; but the international round could be the springboard to a levelling out of the playing field. The idea that foreign fans could adopt unfashionable clubs en-masse is not so unbelievable. During the World Cup in Korea/Japan whole countries were adopted by towns and cities; Wigan could yet twin with Woggawogga.

***

As long as all the revenue from the 39th game is equally distributed then it can be a force for good. Manchester United recently played a testimonial match in mid-January and received a £1m fee. Based on that figure surely an average of £10m per match for 10 competitive games could be achieved. In these days when rich men spend millions on their children's weddings – including hiring chart topping pop stars, these kind of numbers are achievable. This suggests that an extra £5m of revenue could be raised for every club before the soft benefits of extra exposure, sponsorship and long-term fan base extension are equated.

On the basis of £5m per club, if the clubs used half of this money to reduce Premier League ticket prices then every top flight club could reduce prices by £2 - £5 per game; this is one way that match going fans could actually benefit.

Alternatively the clubs could canvass the fans on what they wanted the £5m spent on – transfers, debts, reduced ticket prices, cheaper beer whatever; it is possible to engage the fans on this issue.

The Premier League, for all its faults, is far fairer than Serie A or Primera Liga in terms of distributing television revenue and prize money. The Spanish system almost guarantees the Barca/Real duopoly and Juve/Inter/Milan use their own TV season tickets, disconnected from the larger Serie A community to embed bigger revenue streams. If all the proceeds from these game were shared evenly, then the possibility of £5m per club for a one-off game would boost the smaller clubs more than the bigger ones. It might then actually tighten the division up. Reduced prices would put more fans into, say, Middlesbrough's stadium that any of the top sides; simply because the top grounds are already full.

***

The international round proposal does need some work to make it a more viable proposal; and one of the areas that would need working on is the seeding aspect. Why is there a need for the top five sides to be seeded to keep them apart?

If the games were played between teams next to each other in the table then they would be more competitive and therefore unbalance the league less. If Manchester United play Derby whereas Fulham play Reading and Chelsea play Tottenham, there is an obvious imbalance. Surely it would be better if Chelsea played Manchester United and Derby played Birmingham - both games would be competitive and surely that is a fairer basis to start. West Ham would obviously get to play Tottenham more often than not - so there are pros and cons.

On top of this if the games were considered to be like mini-tours then teams would not need to take their players out of the country for warmer climes as a holiday (with the odd match for the sponsors thrown in). Instead clubs could escape and play a competitive match in January somewhere warm – this would certainly be appreciated by a lot of the fair-weather players! A January break has long been mooted as a possibility and this game could become part of it; alternatively play the international round as the first game of the season. The Community Shield weekend could easily be replaced by an international round and would help start the season off with a bang.

And whilst nothing is yet decided the game could be played differently. What about if no points were awarded for winning, drawing or losing - but the goals scored and conceded counted. The players could play fast and loose, and if this was pre-season the managers could try out a few players or new tactics without too much damage.

***

The 39th Game: Premier League plays at imperialism

Arsene Wenger was an early advocate of the international round of matches:

"... a lot of people are coming out against it, without analysing it, and the English Premier League is trying to do something for the fans who are abroad, which I like. That the English Premier League wants to be dominant in the world, I like that as well - because I am a part of it! So, I think there are a lot of plusses as well."

Wenger repeated his thoughts that the game would take the Premier League to the '90%' of fans outside England; in fact Wenger was broadly suggesting that this was fair on the fans. He has since suggested that the plan is dead:

"The idea looks to be dead, maybe because the idea came out in a brutal way and maybe the PR was not done.

"Now it looks to be an idea which is in a very difficult position.

"I was open-minded but as well I will not cry if it doesn't happen. I just felt there was something to explore there which will now not be done.

"It looks difficult to resurrect now because Uefa, Fifa and The FA have come out against it. It is a big stream to swim against now."

Avram Grant also backed the concept that the Premier League should go global, even if he had concerned about this specific proposal:

The 39th Game: Premier League plays at imperialism

"There are many supporters of the Premier League abroad that maybe deserve one time of the year to see it live, then I don't think it is a bad idea, we need to be open and I cannot say 100 per cent that it is a good idea, but we need to think about it."

The idea that the Premier League has fans outside of England is not a revelation; what is interesting is that key decision makers in the English game take them very seriously. The situation has moved quite a distance away from a pre-season tour lasting a week or two; now tournaments are played for much of the summer and players paraded in front of adulatory crowds. Is there a reasonable argument to suggest that allowing some of the fans the chance to see their heroes in a truly competitive match is only fair? The world moves on and the Premier League is probably the only truly global league – with players on show from dozens of different countries from every populated continent. Why shouldn't fans in far-flung cities watch Manchester United or Chelsea or Middlesbrough in the flesh once a year?

***

The first alternative, to change, that always springs to mind is to do nothing, but as the Premier League has demonstrated that option will no longer be acceptable to the money men attracted to the unfettered governance of the Premier League. By 2020 the Premier League will have evolved further - the only real question is how the evolution happens and who hopes to benefit.

The 39th Game: Premier League plays at imperialism

Whilst other sports have played league games on neutral grounds (Rugby League has, as usual, pioneered this idea to extend its geographical reach – as has American Football), football hasn't. If the Premier League doesn't try it then Serie A or Primera Liga will. Possibly FIFA would have a few thoughts on further international club games on top of their International Clubs' Cup; Sepp Blatter has been very vocal in his opposition to Game 39. And then English football may have to play catch-up using rules decided elsewhere. And playing catch-up will probably be less lucrative and less beneficial. Make no mistake the most nervous people in world football about this idea are the movers and shakers at the likes of Milan and Real Madrid.

If the Premier League doesn't act while it is the biggest and best league it runs the risk that when the Italians or Germans or Spanish or (unlikely though it sounds) the French take their turn at the trough then they will take bold action. Perhaps an extra league game is the wrong answer to the question of internationalisation; and that a cup competition may be a more appropriate response. There is little doubt that FIFA would fight such an alternative tooth-and-claw to protect the supremacy of their International Club competition. But after the jolt of an international league game, fans may well be softened up sufficiently to offer little resistance to a cup tournament, possibly one that replaces the severely devalued Football League Cup – International Premier League Cup anyone?

There is always the uncomfortable prospect of a European Super League as an alternative. And quite frankly a European Super League is a bad thing; it would denude the domestic game of the top teams and best players and leave the rump fighting it out for a devalued competition. This measure could be a step that might avert a bigger break-away and still increase revenue. One game away is not too bad considering most top flight teams try to get their players away for a week or two over the tough winter months in any event.

There seems little doubt that the Premier League expected little opposition to its plan, and that whatever opposition was forthcoming would be quickly brushed away. But given the strength and depth of the objections to the 39th game the proposal currently looks doomed. The 39th game proposal may well be eventually abandoned and stuck in the bin with the European Cup Winners' Cup and the Anglo-Italian Cup. Or it could merely be stuck on a shelf sandwiched between a financial analysis of a European Super League and a white paper arguing for a revival of Grange Hill.

But regardless of how its likely abandonment this summer is reported this will not be the last attempt by the Premier League to try to cash in on the 90% of the fans of Premier League that live outside of England; in years to come this interesting, if flawed proposal, may come to be seen as the catalyst for change in the Premier League that is even less palatable.

Chapter 4: The 39th game would be a bad move

by Stephen Orford

"This is abuse. The rich Premier League is trying to get richer and wants to expand the importance of that league."
Sepp Blatter - FIFA President

On October 28 2007 the soon-to-be Superbowl champion New York Giants took on the already hapless and to that point winless Miami Dolphins at Wembley Stadium, London.

Yes. Wembley Stadium. London. Not New York, New York as someone famous once sang, nor Miami, Florida. London, England. Few can recall the score although anyone in the know about the NFL will be aware that the Giants emerged from the Wembley swamp with the 'W'. What was more important than New York's 13-10 victory that day was that this was the first regular season NFL game played outside of North America.

Guardians of a superb but misunderstood product, the NFL's great and good justified their overseas jaunt by insisting that they wanted to spread the word about their game. A sport as laden with cash as any other which immediately springs to mind had, according to its officials, finally succumbed to the need to expand into foreign territories. It had absolutely nothing to do with cash. Got that? Nothing.

Cynics sneered and huffed in equal measure. They pointed to the fact that the NFL had been running successfully and profitably for some 80 years in isolation, and scarcely needed to impress anyone from abroad. So what if this was a sport never destined to be globally viable enough to be included in the Olympic Games or to stage a World Cup? Sports fans are only interested in their local or state sides in any case. Right? And if the world isn't interested then what the heck? We'll just lavish the Super Bowl champions with the title 'World Champions' and be done with it.

Quite how much cash was accrued as a result of the Wembley exercise is unclear. Plenty, would be a ballpark estimate. Certainly enough to justify the trip regardless of how many new and committed fans were attracted to the sport long-term. What is clear is that 81,176 hardy souls braved the lashing rain in the English capital, even enduring one of the sport's uglier games just to feel part of the experience. It is said that replica shirts of all 32 teams were on show on Wembley way before kick-off, and that all in all a wonderful time was had by all. With the possible exception of the still winless Dolphins.

At a very big push it is conceivable that the NFL's motives are pure. That they have woken from their 80-plus year slumber and decided to offer their game to the world. If globalisation of a sport is desirable, then few sports are more in need of a Michael Palin-style trek around the planet than American Football. There'll be more, as over the next three years the NFL have committed to staging one regular game per season in the UK, with the San Diego Chargers and the New Orleans Saints the next duo scheduled to sample NFL the London way in October 2008. What price the winner going on to win the Super Bowl and the loser earning the dubious honour of the first draft choice ahead of 2009?

In addition to a schedule of Wembley dates that would make Robbie Williams jealous, the League is also set to approve the Buffalo Bills' plans to stage several of their home games in Toronto, Canada over the next five seasons. If the NFL keep marketing their product abroad with this kind of aggression there will surely be an American Football World Cup by 2020. Perhaps we're jumping the gun. They'd have to work on the title in any case.

As with all things American we Brits are not too far behind. Just as 'Coupling' followed hot on the heels of 'Friends' and Tony followed Dubya into Iraq, so the English Premier League officials are examining the possibility of taking their product on the road. Premier League chief executive Peter Scudamore proudly announced plans for member clubs to fulfill a 39th fixture, the venue of which might be Beijing, Bangkok, Sydney or Los Angeles, but certainly not Islington or Trafford. Again the reasoning offered was the need to expand the product to a global audience, an apparently noble aim even if it the intended format can only distort the competition.

Run that by us again, Mr Scudamore? You want to globalise football? FIFA, football's world governing body, currently has 208 member associations across all five continents. These associations include the countries identified as possible hosts of the Premier

League's imaginatively titled 'international round'. For those of you not watching in Premierleaguevision HD those potential hosts are China, Thailand, Australia and the United States of America. That said, who exactly will Scudamore and company be singing their tuneless gospel song to?

Potential Premier League fans, that's who. Seemingly, this is also the same audience that the Premier League's rich-set (otherwise known as the top or 'Big' four) would like to capture. If all 32 NFL teams were represented by way of replica jerseys at Wembley last October, then how many Manchester United, Arsenal, Liverpool or Chelsea shirts will disappear from shelves in Chicago, Shanghai, Melbourne or Chiang Mai? Even their Russian connections won't be enough to stop Chelsea becoming fashionable stateside if the Stamford Bridge club promise that Frank, Didier and JT will show up every January to entertain the masses.

The idea for an international round is one almost certainly stolen from yet another sport with a greater need to self publicise than football. Over the weekend of May 5 and 6 2007 all six scheduled Super League fixtures were played at Cardiff's Millennium Stadium. This was part of the sport's relentless and often embarrassing crusade to establish a Super League club in staunch Rugby Union territory. Six exciting games and two days of cordial jollity later the event was pronounced an unqualified success by the self same people who organised it, and a repeat is planned for the May Day Bank Holiday weekend in 2008. Dubbed 'Millennium Magic', the event is likely to become a permanent fixture in the domestic rugby league calendar, and may even continue to be so when the Celtic

Crusaders take their inevitable place in the newly franchised top-flight.

Yet the circumstances for the Premier League's plans differ dramatically from those which inspired the bigwigs at the Rugby Football League. After the initial and almost overwhelming sound of collective baulking from top (Big) four managers at the prospect of playing a major title rival on neutral ground, Scudamore hinted quite forcefully that the issue of who plays who will be determined according to a seeding system. This will be no 'Grand Slam Sunday'. Perhaps the Premier League have realised that nobody outside the UK will believe that the top (Big) four were randomly selected by a fixture computer to play each other on the same day twice a season. Nobody believes it in Super League either, but we would all rather watch close sporting contests, however suspiciously arranged, than one-sided wallopings.

The "39th Step" will not have intense competition at the top of its list of motives. Instead we will most likely get a series of Big Guy v Little Guy clashes which, by 2010 or 2011 will offer even less chance of a surprise result than they do now. If the Premier League wishes to advertise it's wares beyond these shores, why does it seek to do it with mismatches? Indeed, shouldn't it first be working towards a method of eradicating mismatches altogether before it goes out of its front door, much less on the road? In 2007/08 Premier League basement club Derby County have shipped in six goals in a game on three occasions and five on two more. They are set for a record low number of points in the Premier League's brief history, and have won just once all season. With the gap between the top flight and the Championship growing it is likely that teams promoted from the Championship's end of season play-offs in the future will suffer similarly.

That issue is perhaps for another day, but for now consider the possibility of how many will be attracted to see Manchester United meet Fulham in Mumbai, or Arsenal take on Wigan Athletic in Cape Town. There have already been dissenting noises from the associations of those nations ear-marked for a visit:

"We'll vote strongly against it. The Premier League is putting money before responsibility and dignity."

Offered Asian Confederation president Mohamed bin Hammam, while United States Football's top man Sunil Gulati chipped in:

"We've been reluctant to have official games played in the US. We'll be guided by Fifa on this matter. But if it's not in line with its rules then we won't sanction it."

Most damningly of all, Japanese FA vice-president Jungi Ogara declared:

"It sounds problematic. We are, in principle, opposed to having Premier League games in Japan as we have to protect our league and clubs."

And Football Federation Austrialia chief executive Ben Buckley added:

The 39th Game: Premier League plays at imperialism

"Football Federation Australia's overwhelming priority is to promote the Hyundai A-League and to continue to invest in, and grow, the game in Australia."

All of which rather pokes Scudamore and company in the metaphorical eye, and brings us to the question of whether it is necessarily a good thing for countries who already have their own professional leagues and national teams to be inhabited by fanatical supporters of mega-rich, increasingly soulless Superclubs. How much stronger might the leagues of Ireland and Wales be were it not for the fact that most of the population of those countries would rather travel to England or Scotland in search of more immediate success? The Premier League and its more affluent members may not be deterred from their quest for world domination by this thought, but a monopoly on worldwide fan interest is almost certainly not what prompted Robert Guerin and company to form FIFA more than 100 years ago.

Even those apparently yet to be introduced to Premier League football (there must be some, somewhere eh Mr Scudamore?) are probably aware that the English national team has got the summer off in 2008. England's cataclysmic failure to qualify for Euro 2008 was greeted with widespread anger and derision by the written press, and a shrug of the shoulders by the Premier League. Yet in their apathy they could be doing more to promote Team England than they might imagine.

If is not the case already, a series of games staged in continents beyond Europe could ensure that all fans in hitherto unfashionable football outposts become Big four devotees, just as we have seen in

Ireland and much of Wales. In turn the teams in their own less popular domestic leagues will be utterly deserted and ignored, resulting in an economic and therefore sporting climate which makes it impossible for emerging nations to prosper on the international stage. If you can't beat the opposition with technical and tactical innovation, suppress them with your extremely large wallet. If only we'd thought of that when the Mighty Magyars were in town in the 1950's.

Among those within the game the main bone of contention with the idea has been it's potential effect on the integrity of the competition. An extra game, or "39th step" as it is now commonly known in football circles entirely distorts the format of the Premier League. Since time immemorial the basic principle of a league fixture list within the sport of football is that all teams involved will meet each other twice. Traditionally, teams will play one of these games at home and one away. When the Football League was formed in 1888 nobody mentioned anything about playing an extra game. Certainly not in Congo at any rate.

While there has been much tinkering with the format since the Football League's inception (two points for a win, various changes to the number of clubs promoted and relegated from any division, and changes to the number of teams which make up a division among them), it has always been a reasonable assumption that the fixture list will have a certain symmetry about it, and that all games should take place on UK soil. An extra game immediately unbalances the whole league programme and offers unfair advantages to some while dishing out unfair punishments to others. Who is going to get the short straw that is having to play

The 39th Game: Premier League plays at imperialism

Manchester United or Arsenal after a 25-hour flight to Adelaide? Who will be lucky enough to make the relatively short hop to New York ahead of a crunch clash with our whipping boy friends from Derby County? Or their future equivalent? And there will be one. Increasingly in the Premier League, there always is. Be it Sunderland, Swindon Town or Sunderland (again), there seems always to be a team who can be relied upon to perform in an utterly abject manner.

The Premier League chiefs are not deterred by this imbalance, and once again it is our friends in Super League who set the dangerous precedent. Super League is currently a competition comprising 12 clubs, yet runs for 27 'regular season rounds' before the commencement of the all-important and pre-1998 non-existent 'playoffs' and 'Grand Final'. Leaving the debate about the merits of a playoff system aside for now, how do 12 clubs fulfil 27 fixtures each? Duplication is the simple answer. At the behest of the rugby league administrators top flight clubs are required to play each other once at home and once away, before making up the rest of their programme with extra fixtures against sides closest to them in the previous season's league standings. All of which leads to umpteen St Helens v Wigan, Bradford v Leeds or Warrington v Hull clashes, the majority of which even this resident and ardent fan of St.Helens struggles to remember. It's reasonable to assume that it is a similar story for the fans of Leeds and Bradford, Hull and Warrington, and even Johnny-come-lately upstarts like Catalans and Harlequins and so on and so forth.

The reason given for this strange state of affairs is not dressed up as anything other than the need for more money through the turnstiles for the clubs. Unlike the Premier League's privileged members most rugby league clubs operate on the proverbial shoestring and so need extra revenue from gate receipts to maximise their income potential. All of which has practically murdered the international game before it has even begun, with no space in an already packed schedule for even the merest whiff of a rugby union-style five or six nations tournament. While the Premier League still has to accommodate international football at least on the calendar (how long for is a question for another chapter, or even another book), it can only harm the international game by taking a 39th step. Such a step is certain to stifle rather than enhance development elsewhere, unbalance a competition format more than a century old, and place yet more demands on players who are already being flogged like slaves according to their worried club managers. Although there were rather less multi-millionaires among the slave population all those years ago. It's clear that neither the Premier League nor its competitors actually need the extra revenue this would bring, so we can only assume that a ravenous greed is the principal motive.

However mention of the demand on the players brings us nicely on to another reason why opinion from Premier League managers is at best split over this issue. Since the Champions League came into being in the mid-1990's we have been hearing about how the extra games from the league format are contributing to player burn-out. Managers have responded by resting players for games they perceive to be less important, resulting in a widely held belief that not only the Carling or League Cup is now devalued, but also that the same fate has befallen the FA Cup. Those with a glass half full consider this year's final between Portsmouth and Cardiff City to be an exciting throwback to the days when the FA Cup was 'The Thing', in an era when any club could begin a season with a realistic dream that this could be 'their year'. Yet those of a glass half empty persuasion consider the loss of, you guessed it, THOSE FOUR in the early rounds (and in the case of Chelsea and Liverpool against lower league opposition) to be an indication that the great old competition is devalued beyond redemption.

For those people the cup's nadir came in 2000 when holders Manchester United pulled out of the defence of their trophy under pressure from FIFA to attend a World Club Championship tournament in Brazil. Since that day, and with the increasing financial pressure on clubs to stay in the Premier League taking effect, even mid-ranking top-flight clubs seem to be able to find better uses of their time than making a genuine effort to win club football's most famous prize. Thus players are rested, fans are short-changed and the cup ends up in need of a good hard polish if it is to restore its shine. In the 2007/08 tournament the likes of Blackburn Rovers, Bolton Wanderers, Fulham and Derby County among others have been dumped out early after fielding weakened sides. If even they don't care, how can we be surprised when top four chasers Everton and Liverpool are dumped out by Oldham Athletic and Barnsley respectively?

A 39th Premier League game would only place more demands on top-flight players, and persuade their managers to employ more of the kind of squad rotation that is the scourge of the modern game in both the league and cup competitions. With important games either side of the 39th step, would Sir Alex Ferguson or Arsene

Wenger even bother to field a full-strength team in the international round if the Premier League acceded to their demands and gave their teams a softer fixture?

Frankly it could either way. At a push the Premier League managers might be persuaded to buy in to the 39th step and send out the superstars for the occasion. Yet with the extra date on the calendar another game would suffer somewhere along the line of a busy season. Players would likely be rested on their return meaning that regular paying customers would be getting less than their money's worth next time out. And what if a player suffered a serious injury while engaged in the 39th step? Will those club managers who have initially raised their concerns about the idea then want to be compensated when the inevitable happens? I recall something similar happening to Colin Montgomorie ahead of a major golf tournament not so long ago. He was not compensated as it was his own fault, but then he didn't need the money any more than Manchester United or Liverpool do.

Of course if you believe those behind the 39th step concept it is not about the money. It is about introducing fans across the globe to the English game. Yet it seems the two parties have already met. Millions already watch Premier League television coverage around the world, and are brainwashed into believing copious amounts of hyperbole about an admittedly strong but hardly flawless product. Television and radio presenters are constantly telling us that the English Premier League has now overtaken both the Spanish La Liga and the Italian Serie A as the best league in the world. Quite how this curious and slightly dubious title is judged is a little cloudy, but if you tell your audience enough times they will start to believe it. It's the same kind of principal upon which Dubya and Tony based their arguments for marching blindly, illegally into Iraq. The difference is that Sunderland v Wigan Athletic is not so much a smoking gun as a simmering, slightly flagging sparkler at the end of Guy Fawkes Night. Played at it's very highest level the English Premier League is indeed a fantastic product, the equal of any other. Yet those behind the 39th step would do well to remember that the league lacks true depth.

All of which leaves little appetite among the match-going fans for an extra game in some far flung corner of the globe. Travel costs, transport arrangements, political objections (if Beijing is not a fit host for the Olympic Games then what makes Scudamore and his cronies think it is acceptable to take Arsenal v West Ham United to Shanghai?), squad rotations, potential player burn-out, mismatches and a better than even chance of harming the English national team are not the attributes which attract your average Premier League fan to a new concept. They'd all rather be watching their own team, in their own stadium, and file out to their own local pub afterwards. Or should that now be their own team, in their own armchair, or their own local pub? Either way there is much to be said for a match day routine, and surely some traditions should be left alone.

For now the usually controversial FIFA President Sepp Blatter agrees. There seems little immediate prospect of FIFA sanctioning overseas Premier League matches for all of the reasons outlined here. Oh, and because UEFA's newest mover, shaker and rent-a-quote legend Michel Platini doesn't much fancy the idea either. If Scudamore and the Premier League plan to ride roughshod over the wishes of the game's international governing bodies they are displaying an arrogance that even their fiercest critics might have thought beyond them. Yet worryingly, the more money that pours into the English game from television, the more invincible the Premier League believes itself to be. Scudamore appeared to offer a climbdown following the reaction to the idea from FIFA and UEFA, but you get the feeling that he has only retreated temporarily. Like Darth Vader spinning around in outer space at the end of the first Star Wars movie, the Empire is likely to strike back in its quest to rule the world.

Chapter 5: 39th Game Has Logic

By Hugh Larkin

"This is a chance for the Premier League to showcase its product around the world"
Mihir Bose BBC Sports Editor 7 Feb 2008

The reason the Premier League's International round is so controversial is also why it might be a huge success if it gets off the ground.

The critical element in the 39th game plan is that the matches played on overseas soil would count toward the final standings in the Premiership table. These would be meaningful games in which the competing sides can be expected to give their all and put out full strength selections.

Premiership sides have periodically played exhibition matches abroad and have even begun to make these trips during the active season-Manchester United only recently went to the Middle East during the current campaign. It's not difficult to see why; they make a lot of cash for one game.

The 39th Game: Premier League plays at imperialism

Pre-season friendlies have always been a key part of the soccer calendar and over the past decade elite clubs have increasingly used overseas tournaments as part of their preparation

The problem is that everyone knows that a pre-season four team event in South Korea isn't a priority for the clubs in terms of winning and increasingly fans in Asia- but also the USA- are not that impressed.

It used to the case that the sight of European or South American stars would be enough to bring out the regular soccer fans, plus a whole bunch of spectators curious to see what all the fuss was about.

In the modern age, television and the media has brought the game to nearly every corner of the planet and while this has provoked new interest it has also removed the novelty value.

No longer is the average fan in Asia, North America or Australasia just going to be grateful to have a live view of the top players. Television will show them weekly the difference between the invitation matches they watch and the shuddering collisions in Premiership or Champions League.

To use marketing speak, the brand has established itself so well that there is huge demand for the product but for the real thing, not a substitute.

On a wider stage, the Continents outside Europe are far more confident of their economic wealth and have awareness that their spending power can provide more control over the global game. The example of cricket is there for all to see.

So the Premier League's 39th game plan has a tremendous logic about it. If there is going to be expansion into new territories it has to be done with a meaningful product, otherwise the new markets aren't going open up.

Alternatives have been suggested but some have insurmountable problems caused by organisation and others just have a patronising air about them.

The Community Shield is one match that has been mooted for delivery to an overseas venue. This year's FA Cup has pointed up the biggest problem with that idea. There is every chance that the 2008 game could have been a mismatch between, say, Manchester United and Barnsley - not easy to market in Shanghai, Melbourne or Los Angeles. As it was there would have been difficulties marketing Portsmouth versus Cardiff to an international audience.

Even if the line up was to be the usual head-to-head between two of the 'Big 4', there's no getting away from the truth that this is a glorified friendly. How many supporters really care who wins it, even among fans of the competing sides?

In addition, the Premier League can ill afford to annex a game to their global expansion plans that has its origins in the sport trying to raise money for charity. It has huge potential for another PR own goal.

Another idea is to have a Cup competition played out between some, or all, of the Premiership sides. This concept immediately hits fixture and sanctioning problems.

The elite clubs, whose participation would surely be demanded to make it appealing, consider that they have enough on their plate already. They already habitually disrespect the Carling Cup but this idea might mean dropping out altogether.

There might be a decent case to make against the Carling Cup but the Football League isn't likely to take this kindly- and as UEFA awards a UEFA Cup place to the Cup winner, that would draw the governing body in and open up another front in the battle with those who run European soccer.

Finally, the overarching problem wouldn't be addressed- a 'Premiership Cup' sounds like one more pumped up mini-tournament that neither fans or clubs would rate highly.

A third model is the one used by the NFL who moved a single game of their regular season to London. This is possibly the only option which has a chance next to the 39th game plan.

Two or three selected games could be deployed around the globe but there are many matters to overcome. Firstly, there is the identity of the teams- the punters around the globe are hardly likely to shell out for a visit from Reading and Bolton.

The pressure would be on to send exactly those sides who are most affected by fixture congestion issues in Europe. And the 'Big 4' would baulk at two of them going and two not.

When Manchester United appeared in the World Club in 2000 there was an unholy row about the leeway given to the Red Devils to enable them to fulfil those fixtures. If all the 'Big 4' received the same then the Evertons and Spurs of the chasing pack would surely cry foul.

Another issue is money. The NFL operates a pooled approach to marketing which the Premiership doesn't. At the moment the participants in games allocated abroad could make extra cash denied to those not selected. Given the way Premiership clubs tend to behave, it would be a surprise to see the 'Big 4' agree to fly around the globe to make money for their rivals.

On the surface this looks to be a far less problematic expansion plan than the 39th game plan but in reality it causes as many issues for less gain.

The 39th Game advocates certainly have logic on their side. Once the argument that the Premier League should play overseas is conceded (and that debate is covered elsewhere in this book), involving all 20 clubs becomes the simplest move.

With Premiership sides flying the world to take part in mini-competitions and exhibitions there is little point in trying to lay more glorified friendlies on to the paying public on other Continents.

There is an appetite for the chance to watch a full-blooded League game and the marketing mean would have something tangible to sell. On the face of it the 39th Game appears a very ambitious, even greedy concept but actually the Premier League have it right- if the competition is going to become global, better to do it properly than in a half-hearted manner.

Chapter 6: Eating at the top table

By Colin Illingworth, Antony Melvin

Nothing profits more than self-esteem, grounded on what is just and right.
John Milton

We've canvassed views of a number of official and unofficial supporters groups, season ticket holders, lifelong fans and some key internet fansites and bloggers to come up with a combined view of fans of the Premier League clubs; interestingly their views are as varied as their clubs - and not totally opposed (although somewhat opposed in general). The views expressed can in no way reflect the mood of the club involved or all the fans of any of the clubs mentioned, but are included to give a snapshot of the reaction to the proposal in its formative stages.

The first block of fans are drawn from the financially powerful teams, the seven teams that have been ever-present in the Premier League and have been able to access ever larger buckets of cash as a result. This covers Arsenal, Aston Villa, Chelsea, Everton, Liverpool, Manchester United and Tottenham Hotspur. Added to this elite group are the teams newly acquired by billionaires who could therefore bridge the financial gap; Newcastle United and Manchester City.

These comments are extendable; if you want to contribute to this section please send your comments plus the team that you support to editor@squarefootball.net - and we will look to include the best comments in future revisions of the book.

Arsenal

Arsenal fan **Christina Ruse** claims Mr Scudamore's plan would make a *"mockery of the current league system"* **and fears** that this could signal the start of a new breakaway league:

> *"The gap between the super rich clubs and the others within the Premiership is getting wider and wider. This idea will fuel that. Maybe that's the scam – to use this overseas game idea to shrink the Premiership in order to make room for overseas fixtures so that the Premier League becomes a world Super League involving only half a dozen clubs from here. Then the other clubs would be encouraged to slip back into the Championship which must then divide because it would be too big . . . We end up with a Super League, a new Premiership, a Championship etc. Is this the underlying Scudamore plan?"*

Christina believes that if the money-hungry chairmen aren't careful they risk destroying the game and the return of the hooligan element that plagued the English game in the 70s and 80s:

The 39th Game: Premier League plays at imperialism

"To me this is ONLY a financial move to benefit the top five super-rich Premiership clubs. These are the only games that would fill stadiums overseas. But, having lived overseas for years, my fundamental opposition is that such an idea is insulting to the development of their own football. I'm delighted that this is Japan's view (that they are not interested in staging such a fixture), maybe the view of all Asia. It smacks of neo-colonialism. It is possible to watch every game by these big UK clubs on TV.

"Fans at games here are becoming unimportant – we already feel that because of rising ticket prices, fixtures like League Cup and FA Cup coming off season tickets, ridiculous food/drink prices, seeing 'club level' libraries where people stay drinking/eating inside for a good percentage of games. We'll end up (soon!) with half-filled stadiums like Italy without atmosphere and attracting more of the hooligan element than the true fan – and that's when the 'club levels' will begin to empty since they won't want to be associated. Clubs with huge debts after building new stadiums would be bought and sold and there might be financial chaos. Then the 'world's greats' won't want to play here. The Premiership cannot survive on television revenue alone. They need atmospheric games, rivalry, and passion. Revenue for the development of football outside the top clubs is obviously unimportant in this proposal.

"As a fan I am appalled. Very, very few fans have the money to fly around the world and certainly not to see pointless fixtures. This isn't anything to do with us. It's to do with money. I've already said, continue to alienate us and the traditional fanbase will wilt even more than it has done over the past two years.

Manchester United, Arsenal, Liverpool etc may still get bums on seats but even they know the fanbase is changing fast and so is the atmosphere. I think that unless the 'club level' concept is matched by an area with cheaper, probably standing, fans, atmospheres and traditional rivalry will disappear and people will watch games on TV only. Then just maybe the clubs will begin to take us seriously again. Without us, footie is dead."

It is easier to find Arsenal advocates of the 39th game if you spread your net towards the anonymous '90%' as Arsenal fan **P Sharma**, of North Vancouver, BC, Canada, stated on TimesOnline:

"I live in Canada and have followed the EPL since the 80s. I shall be first in line to buy tickets . . . while I understand the reaction of the English fans they have to accept that globalisation has made their game – and their teams – a global league and global teams. We love our teams (I shall forever be a proud Gooner) as much as you do . . ."

Aston Villa

Vice-chairman of the Aston Villa Supporters Club New York **Donal Neligan** has been a Villa fan since he was six years old and plans his weekends around the fixtures, but although this plan would bring the Villans to him he is also totally against it:

"The top division of English football has a very unique and historic identity that dates back to its founding over a century ago. As Aston Villa fans we feel a strong attachment to this tradition as

it was our own director William McGregor who founded the football league in 1888. Since that time there has been very little change in the league structure even with the founding of the Premier League in 1992 the format has remained the same.

"Over the course of 120 years through two World Wars, the invention of radio and television, English football has grown but retained its identity, I think it should continue to do so and this plan would destroy that identity.

"It could be the start of a very slippery downward slope for the big clubs. If the top sides continue to detach themselves from their grassroots fanbases to becoming more profitable businesses then we very well could see a mass exodus towards the more traditional lower leagues. At first there would be little to notice, the top clubs would continue selling seats to tourists and glory hunters but over time the interest would fade and these super clubs could find their new support vanishing as quickly as they appeared while the old fans they sold out have ventured to pastures new never to return."

Chelsea

It's not just those at the foot of the table who are against the scheme. Father and son Chelsea fans **David and Philip Smith**, from the Chelsea West Midlands supporters club, said they found the proposal totally unfair.

"We are totally against the so-called "39th Step" idea as it goes against the idea of a fair and equally contested league in which every club plays all the others in that division twice, home and away. It would also take games away from the main fans, who reside in this country, often in the town or city where the club is situated/that it represents. The whole idea would be unfair on those clubs fighting relegation places or European competition places as the extra games could change whether a club is successful or loses out.

"The rumoured seeding of the bigger clubs would add to the unfairness of the games as it would reduce Premiership and relegation deciders to being decided by the luck of the draw. What if the famous end of season decider between Liverpool and Arsenal in the 1989 for the league championship had been followed by a "39th Step" match? The excitement of that game would have been lost and the champions could have been decided by the luck of the draw, which we believe would devalue the competition.

"We believe that the claims made about Serie A or La Liga jumping in first are ridiculous as the position of FIFA and UEFA on such matters has always seemed to be clear: it is against their rules."

Rob Hobson, editor of the unofficial Chelsea website www.cfcnet.co.uk is not a fan of the idea:

"If my club/the Premier League suggested to me that I should travel 12,000 miles to watch a London derby, I'll cheerfully do what the club has been trying to do to all of us over the last few years. I'll stop going and I'll have a relationship with my television instead."

Fellow Chelsea fans David and Philip Smith agreed:

"As fans, we would be disgusted if this went ahead and we would be less inclined to go to games. We would certainly not go abroad to watch the games and would probably be put off watching games on TV as we do now as it would turn the competition into a last-minute lottery. We think the idea would kill the English game as the fans would revolt. None of our friends who support Chelsea or other rival teams have been in favour of the idea. We just don't believe that it will ever happen."

But again for an alternative view you need to trawl the relative anonymity of online feedback at sites like TimesOnline. Another Chelsea fan, **J Best** from Waterlooville, left his views there and basically suggested that we've only got ourselves to blame.

"Sorry guys but my team hasn't been a "local" team for years. The chairman is a Russian with a business in France most of our best players are from the African nations. Every player bar two have been bought in from other clubs in the last two years. Nothing local about that and if the foreign owners decide they want to increase their investment who are we, who welcomed them with open arms when they can in to save our clubs from going bankrupt, to deny them that right? We cheerfully pay through the nose to watch players who have no connection with *our teams, clubs or cities, other than as employees, perform each week and they also have the right to move around to get the best deal. It really is only theatre now so let the impresarios who foot the bill have the freedom to maximise their profits."*

However, Rob Hobson, who has no problem with clubs going to Asia and America for non-competitive games, believes that the plan could actually have an adverse effect.

"Anyone forced to sit through the stultifying dull 0-0 draw between Chelsea and Liverpool this season probably wished themselves violently somewhere else – I know I did! If I were a native of, say, Miami or Taiwan, those 90 minutes alone would probably drive me irretrievably to a sport with a little more oomph. Curling springs to mind."

Everton

Mr Scudamore does have a few supporters of his plan. Everton fan **Craig Fletcher** had an interesting angle on why this could benefit Everton:

"The whole KEIOC argument is that Everton could have found a new stadium within the city, but the club keep saying it would cost too much. With the extra millions from a scheme like this the club would have no argument to build a stadium in that place (I'm not saying it) and would have to reconsider and build one close to its fans. If we want to abandon the city to the other lot, then the

80% of Scousers that support Everton will quickly dwindle and we will have sold our heritage for a pitch in a Tesco car park. Not every club has masses of money and I'm not so proud that I would turn down a few million quid a year if it kept Everton in the city."

Liverpool

Liverpool fan **Mark Williams** is convinced that the extra fixture would enrich the bigger teams:

"I'm not aware of how receipts will be distributed. But if hosts bid for hosting fixtures, I would guess the big clubs would attract (and therefore demand) a bigger sum, which would of course benefit them more than smaller clubs. (I'm guessing smaller clubs would look for a Cup style draw against a big club, unless they were involved in relegation/qualification.)"

But he is not totally against the possibility of an extra 'away' game:

"If we need to sell our domestic game I'd rather it was outside of the normal league. Either a separate cup competition (although where we'd make the room from I don't know), or play-offs (which could be introduced, Dutch-style) for relegation and Euro places. In principle, no [I don't want league matches played in Beijing], but as a realist who has to some extent already given up on football, I see it as almost inevitable. I do object to an extra

fixture; I think a league should entail everyone playing each other a fixed number of times."

Simon Towers, is another lifetime Liverpool fan is old enough to remember alternating between Everton and Liverpool home games when he first started attending matches in the 1980s. He feels that the plan would benefit the big teams and isn't against the idea in principle.

"Seems fine but needs some thought re level playing field ie next opponents haven't travelled as far and so not as knackered etc could be a couple of weeks spill over on this so careful thought re post match fixtures is needed."

A Liverpool fan by the name of **Norah**, from Singapore, agreed that it goes against everything that football stands for. She left a message on the Timesonline website.

"I live in Singapore and even though, I would give everything to see Liverpool in the flesh for the first time, this is an absolutely terrible idea. It robs the Premier League of everything I imagine it once stood for.

"In my mind, I've always made plans to see my team, my club, in action on their native soil, England. Nowhere else. It just seems like an absolute farce to me...something that no club would take seriously, and that is certainly not what I want to witness when I watch a match."

The 39th Game: Premier League plays at imperialism

Manchester City

Rob Benyon is a City fan with fond memories of the last title win in 1968; but despite any benefit to him he'd rather the traditions remained:

"I have supported Manchester City for the past 64 years! but currently I am living in Florida and only get to see them on tv....which is quite often with them as the game is taking off over here.

"The 39th game proposal is only going to benefit the bigger clubs. I cannot see the likes of Rochdale or Stockport or Bury travelling abroad to play an exhibition game. I think it is about making money; the real beneficiary in my mind would be the United States, where they have the cash and openings for such games.

"I personally cannot see any benefits for British football coming from the 39th game.

"Other countries may take advantage if the English clubs don't participate, but quite honestly the English would have nothing to benefit from a game abroad.

"I would prefer that English clubs attracted foreign opposition in friendlies for the sake of the fans.

"My "general comment" is that the standard of refereeing is not only poor at the moment in the UK because I can see games from Argentina, Spain, Italy, Mexico, and other South American countries, and believe me, the referees are just as good at making the mistakes that the English referees are making."

The 39th Game: Premier League plays at imperialism

Steve Heald, long-time Manchester City fan and Squarefootball writer, but currently disillusioned, was prepared to set out his agenda for making the plan work;

PLAY THE GAMES IN AUGUST

"Abolish the Community Shield and take a percentage cut from the 39th games to recoup the money for good causes. All the teams are on pre-season tours and could tailor this game to their schedule. After the game all teams still have 38 games home and away to re-coup the lost 3 points. Plus the 39th game doesn't eat into the schedule like the suggested January game would."

NEW HORIZONS FOR FANS

"The loyal travelling supporter will have new and exotic places to visit. With the cheap cost of airline tickets, and the cost of living in the locations meaning ticket prices and refreshments will be considerably lower the games are being played, these games may be no more expensive than Premiership games. With the game being played in August, this trip could be built into the fans summer holiday arrangements."

SEEDING THE GAMES FOR PARITY

"Last seasons league positions would determine who plays who, and there would be a gap of 10 league places in the ties. For example, 1st would play 11th, 2nd versus 12th, 3rd versus 13th, etc. So if the 39th game took place this season, Manchester United as league champions would play Aston Villa, who finished 11th. For the teams promoted to the Premiership the champions

would play last seasons 8th position, which this year would have been Sunderland v Reading. The championship runners-up would play 9th, the play-off winners would play 10th. Everyone would know this going into the end of the season, and there would be extra incentive to finish in the top 10 if you knew you would be facing Derby County (or their ilk) rather than Manchester United by finishing 10th rather than 11th."

HOWEVER...

"When you look at the games that would be played you have to ask who would be interested? As well as the aforementioned Sunderland v Reading tie, based on last season you'd have Fulham v Everton, Blackburn v Derby, and the best one, Bolton v Wigan! As a novelty, you may live in Beijing and go watch one of these games the once, but once you realise the paucity of entertainment these games regularly throw up, and the myth that the Premiership is exciting would be destroyed, I think this idea would sink within a couple of years of its introduction. So therefore, I suggest we bring back the Watney Cup!"

Another City fan and Squarefootball writer, **Dan Bailey**, is dead set against the plan.

"The 39th game is a crucial moment in the long term, and perhaps inevitable, transformation of football from a sport into a business.

"We have already seen shirt-sponsorship ushered in on a grand scale and sky sports revolutionise the game, but the 39th game

The 39th Game: Premier League plays at imperialism

would be the first time in the history of British football that the fundamental and indispensable fairness and equality of the league structure, basic tenants of any sport, would take a back-seat to the pursuit of money.

"Whilst the globalisation of English football could be argued to be a positive progression, could the globalisation of individual clubs be seen in the same light? Perhaps I could be accused of being a Luddite but we should not wish to see the continued erosion of the existing local fan base which these clubs have traditionally been founded upon. It is a process that is already happening at many clubs but it should not be seen on a mass-scale, let alone encouraged by the powers-that-be. The local and loyal supporter has increasingly been slipping down Premier League club's priority lists in favour of more fair-weather 'football tourists', armchair fans, and Sky television. Television revenue accounts for a far greater percentage of club's revenue than what can still be garnered by hard-up fans through ticket sales and merchandise. The 39th game can be seen as the next step on the route away from the hearts of the local community and towards the wallets of the football tourists.

"The 39th game would also signify the 'thin end of the wedge'. Once clubs are regularly playing a proportion of their league games abroad, what is to stop them playing a larger number away from their traditional home? Especially for teams such as Manchester United, who sold out their local, hardcore support in favour of the 'prawn sandwich brigade' years ago, this would be the almost cogent financial culmination of their long-term business structure. What is to stop them dropping the Manchester from their name and simply becoming 'United', a new cosmopolitan brand who tour the world's largest venues every week? Or perhaps, like is commonplace in American Sports and was introduced to the UK by the MK Dons, we will see clubs move location with a far greater frequency, only this time to cities such as Dubai or New York. If league games are regularly being played outside the UK, we would be giving profit-led clubs carte blanche to take the logical next step. At one time we laughed at America's 'franchises' and lauded our own organic, meaningful clubs. Many, including myself were appalled when Wimbledon were 're-branded' as MK Dons. If the 39th game were to be introduced we would be just as likely to see clubs transforming into Sydney Rovers or Washington Villa in the future. My club, Manchester City, would no doubt be fine. It would probably play an increasing number of matches in Bangkok and in financial terms would probably thrive. But would they be MY club anymore?

"To be frank, football 'clubs' haven't been clubs for a long time. We have not been members of a club; we have been the customers of a business and have been treated as such. Even if the rhetoric and club loyalty still exist as a hangover of another era. Football supporters have put up with a great deal over the past 15 years but this would be a step too far and must be opposed.

"The fact that this idea, presented by Premier League Chief Richard Scudamore, initially interested every Premier League chairman unanimously is a depressing thought."

Manchester United

The 39th Game: Premier League plays at imperialism

Some Premier League clubs already make pre-season tours to Asia and the US a priority in order to capture as many new fans as possible. The Premier League even stages a competition in Asia bi-annually and Manchester United recently netted more than a £1 million for an exhibition game in Saudi Arabia. We all know why they really want to forge ahead with the 39th game but **Andy Mitten**, editor of Manchester United fanzine United We Stand, told BBC News 24 that he was worried about where it would all end:

"What if it is a big success? What if Manchester United play a game once a year in Osaka, Melbourne or Dubai and then it becomes more attractive? It is one thing playing a pre-season friendly in Korea, it's another playing Fulham in Seoul in a league match.

"Some Manchester United fans will think it is great but the vast majority will be concerned that football is becoming ever more commercial and that Manchester United, as opposed to Bolton or Fulham, will be forced to trek across to different parts of the world to play games. There will be considerable concern among the fans if there is a trend that leads to the team playing more games away from Old Trafford."

Peter Lee is a season ticket holder and has been a Manchester United fan for the past 32 years and he has strong views on the 39th game. He doesn't believe that the big clubs would necessarily win out.

The 39th Game: Premier League plays at imperialism

"I believe both big and small clubs would benefit in terms of revenue and exposure which will mean clubs can demand more money in sponsorship deals.

"There has been many discussions over the years about how the big clubs play too much football in the Premier League, Champions' League, FA Cup and the Carling cup. There was even talks about reducing the number of clubs in the Premier league. I have some strong reservations about this idea as the preparations prior to a match in a different country are different, for example: travelling time to other side of the world and back again. Acclimatising to the climate of the country, time differences, etc. Stress on players having to be away from family and friends. Furthermore, the 39th game could be against a strong side when your rival side competing for the league could end up playing a lesser side, this is totally unacceptable. Each team should play each equally, at home and away. It is the only fair way.

"The Premiership is already massive and can get enough coverage anyway. It could be that the coverage / exposure / revenues may out weigh the negatives above and then decide to go ahead with it. However, FIFA don't seem too keen on the idea."

And the idea of a match in Beijing left Pete sceptical:

"Beijing may not be a popular choice with their human rights record, but I initially don't like the idea anyway."

Phil MacFarlane, a Manchester United fan from the US, said the Premier League chiefs' sole responsibility should be to ensure that they keep producing entertaining games.

"The Premier League clubs owners should worry about ONE thing – put the most exciting, passionate, attacking, entertaining football out on the pitch every weekend. THAT is what makes them money. THAT is why we watch, pay and support our lads.

"The USA cannot become a football country because the distance alone makes it hard to create the culture of travelling supporters, rivalries, loyalty, let alone chants from the stands. Yes, the rest of the world can grow football, but it will NOT be the English experience."

Much of what season ticket holder, **Jim Frayne**, had to say on the subject was not suitable for a general interest publication; he is clearly another that is against the idea in principle. But he did believe that the Premier League was right to consider options:

"… if the Premier League don't do it, another league will."

Final word from a fan of the team that has done best from the Premier League to date, FSF's **Mark Longden**:

"It's time for us to reclaim our game from those intent on pimping it out just to boost their already burgeoning bank balances."

If Manchester United fans disagree with the proposal – then who will back it?

Newcastle United

Newcastle United fans are famed for travelling the length and breadth of England to follow the Magpies and supporters from the USA have pleaded with the UK-based fans to give them a chance to see their heroes in action in the flesh.

"Carefully planned, this could be a great idea and obviously the chance of watching Newcastle play in the US is a dream for all of us and many a friendship was made when the club last game over here in 2000. As for the fans in the UK – let us have one game a season eh?"

But again the response from a British fan is entirely against the proposal, **Barry Leonard** thinks that the game has forgotten the fans:

"As a season ticket holder at Newcastle United I think the idea of another game played abroad ludicrous. Do they think we have endless amounts of cash just for going to an away game god knows where. How about thinking of the fans for a change instead of just lining their pockets or paying someone £150,000 pound a week it's just gone stupid now.

"The players themselves complain about the amount of games their playing and that we should have a break at xmas. With pre-

season starting earlier every year it will just be continuous with more and more injuries.

"It just smacks of greed from those who wish to endorse it. Please leave our league alone and try and improve the efficiency of our officials and get the game right at home before thinking about taking the circus on tour."

Tottenham Hotspur

In the same week as fans up and down the country put their loyalties aside to pay respect to those who lost their lives in the tragic Munich disaster 50 years ago the timing of the Premier League chief executive's revelation left Tottenham fan **Alberto Contracampo** feeling sick.

"This is just an abomination - when I saw this yesterday my first thought was that football was in danger of losing what little is left of its soul,"

He wrote on the Spurs blog Beef Bagel.

"In a week when football is trying to reserve some dignity with the thoughts of Munich this just disconnects anything that has gone before with today's game what about tradition history etc – this makes it all seem irrelevant. I feel sick."

There is excitement across the globe for the proposal. **Carolyn**, from Perth, Australia, left a comment on the Timesonline website hoping to see Tottenham Hotspur down under.

"Speaking as a huge Tottenham fan (and football fan in general) living in Australia, I think it's an absolutely brilliant idea. Have you any idea how many British ex-pats are living in far flung destinations that would love to have the opportunity to see live Premiership football? Not to mention the legions of Australian and Asian supporters. I would advocate at least giving it a trial run."

But in a developing theme, fans who are British based, like lifelong Spurs fan and Squarefootball writer **Sean O'Meara**, are unimpressed:

"Speaking as a Tottenham supporter, who attends very few games, due mainly to financial constraints and the presence and importance of my young family in my life, I have a clear view on the 39th game proposal.

"The 39th game is an outrageous suggestion, that should be shot down before it is given the chance to even leave the ground.

"To propose that an extra game should be played by each club in the top division is clearly bizarre.

"It is blatantly designed as money spinning idea (which I have yet to hear denied), and most definitely with the good of the bigger clubs in mind, rather than the good of the game, or the supporter.

The 39th Game: Premier League plays at imperialism

"Quite how it is fair for each club to play another random match in a season, against possibly a top or bottom side is frankly nonsense. To be relegated in a season having had to play one of the top four sides three times, when your direct rivals have had to play the same side only twice, is beyond ludicrous.

"This idea almost doesn't warrant the discussion we are having.

"Quite why Wigan and Reading would want to travel to the other side of the world to play a Premiership match is an unanswerable question. With all due respect, the ground they played in would be empty, even if they gave tickets away. A top four women's side would probably attract more interest - again, with all due respect.

"One wonders if the option would be available to these teams to actually elect to play the extra match in England, where match profits may actually be in the black.

"There is no good that can come of this nonsense. It cannot even be sold as a marketing ploy, as coverage of the Premiership is surely already more widely available abroad than it is at home anyway.

"I think it highly unlikely that any other country would step in and make this move if we do not. I think this, because a) there is no other League in the World either stupid enough or conceited anough to think their prouct is THAT marketable and b) no other League in the world is THAT marketable.

"This painfully ill conceived and ill founded idea is the brainchild of the very people that are destroying the magic and romance of the game my six year old son loves so dearly.

The 39th Game: Premier League plays at imperialism

"The money in the game is way, way beyond obscene (which is just one of the reasons why I do not frequent Premiership grounds). To watch a Tottenham side draw 1-1 at home to Middlesbrough, and hear the Spurs manager admit that it is hard to motivate his players with so little of the season remaining and his side in a mid table position and already in Europe via a domestic Cup win, is staggering.

"If the players are not motivated by the enormous amounts of pay they are offered to fulfill every mans boyhood dream, then the time has come for us all to pack up and go home.

"Oh, and that's my ball, and I'll be taking it with me."

Chapter 7: Waiting On

By Colin Illingworth, Antony Melvin

They also serve who only stand and wait.
John Milton

While the 'haves' in the Premier League contemplate whether to spend £15m or £20m on that new forward the rest are looking for a good cup run and a comfortable league position. Could the 39th game improve their lot – or will it simply be another way to cut them adrift from the big money?

Birmingham City

Birmingham owner David Gold has been one of the idea's biggest advocates, but Birmingham fan **Philip Glynn** said there were no advantages to such a scheme, especially when:

"the Blues may not be in the Premier League next season".

He added that Gold's comments have turned the club in to a laughing stock:

"The plan has certainly caused a storm. I have spoken to supporters of Championship sides and they just laugh at the idea. Birmingham City are hanging on by their fingernails, it could be irrelevant for them and there is David Gold supporting it, what a laugh."

Blackburn Rovers

One Blackburn Rovers fan, going by the name of **Albacanuck** on the BBC 606 forum, believes it is all down to one thing.

"Everyone and his uncle and his uncle's dog knows the only reason this is being implemented is to MAKE MORE MONEY! Why then does Scudamore and his ilk insult people's intelligence by spewing a bunch of 'horse's put-oots' about "expansion", "beating others to the punch" and "making the likes of Wigan (no disrespect) recognised worldwide"? This simply illustrates just how gullible and naive Scudamore and his colleagues at the EPL think the average football fan is. Why don't they simply tell the truth....it's nothing more than a pure money-grab to boost the profits of EPL clubs (maybe)."

Guy Pearson is a lapsed Blackburn fan, and couldn't be more opposed to the plan:

"Undoubtedly the draw system will be manipulated to [benefit the big clubs more than the smaller ones]. A game abroad is simply unacceptable, who cares if another league does it, it's simply a bad idea."

Bolton Wanderers

Bolton Wanderers are another club whose Premier League status is under threat this season and **David Blackburn**, a Bolton fan and media relations officer for the Bolton Wanderers Supporters Association, described the plan as ridiculous.

"I think it is a joke and looking at the papers recently, I hope that it has been knocked on the head. Rich clubs getting richer and the fact that they were thinking about seeding it so the top five clubs avoid each other is ridiculous. Putting it as an extra league game, with the way it is we could end up for example playing Arsenal three times and being beaten three times and the relegation could hinge on that, why couldn't we play, nothing against them, Fulham instead! It is our domestic competition, no-one else's."

One of Mr Scudamore's reasons for the 39th game was that it had to act before either La Liga or Serie A did it first, but this claim just doesn't sit right with the majority of the fans. David Blackburn, who said he'd follow the Trotters even if they were in the conference, disagrees:

"That's just an excuse. There is no way the Serie A or La Liga would do it. If anyone wants to do it then go for it - I for one would be bored of it."

Derby County

Derby County are destined for the drop this season but chairman of the RamsTrust **Jim Wheeler**, who has only missed a handful of games over the past 30 years, said he hoped fans would turn their back on the proposal.

"It is totally against the principles of a football league, ignores the feelings of true fans and exposes the Premier League for what it is – driven purely by greed. Hopefully fans would turn their back on the greed league and concentrate on real football."

Fulham

There are a significant minority of fans prepared to voice their support for the plan; Fulham fan **Part time Andy** wrote on the official Fulham forum that he would be all up for it.

"I actually think is a good idea, and you can see that other sports are doing it over here, and it works, and helps spread the word. I saw Man United v Barcelona a few years back in New Jersey USA in the brand new Eagles Stadium, and it was absolutely fantastic! (I) Especially loved the tannoy announcements explaining offside decisions, and announcing a

few 'great saves'. Anyway, I digress... I for one would love to pop over to Dubai with the wife to see us play Liverpool or suchlike. Dubai to see us play Birmingham wouldn't be such a draw."

Middlesbrough

Middlesbrough manager Gareth Southgate said he thought the plan was an early April Fool's joke when he was first informed of the scheme and the chairman of the Official Middlesbrough Supporters Club **Sue Gardener** believes the powers that be are not real football fans.

"Football is known around the world and does not need this so-called "promotion", we are doing quite well so far without it, and the Premier League should leave well alone. Are these "powers that be" football-minded? I guess not otherwise they would know and feel what every football fan goes through each season with their team, without all this extra expense and travel to go with it. Then this in turn leads to the question, "do they care what the fans' think? Don't get me wrong here, I am all for English football being available to all fans, no matter where they may be, but not at the expense of the Premiership fans."

Portsmouth

Since the Premier League was created a number of experts have voiced their concerns about the players taking part in too many games compared to their European counterparts – although it doesn't bother them travelling around the world for a few million on their terms. However secretary of the London Portsmouth Supporters Club **Dan Taylor** finds the idea to include another game, somewhere on earth, "sheer lunacy" and fears for the future of the national team.

"Sadly I think the proposal represents all that is wrong with the Premier League (it's not the land of milk and honey everyone is promised when staring up at it from the lower levels of English football), in as much as it's all about the money rather than the fans. It also strikes me that the proposal seems to run counter to one of the biggest debates when it comes to the national team, which is whether we ask our highly paid idols to play too many games each season. The Premier League was, in a very small way, sanctioned by the FA because the original plan was to reduce the number of top flight clubs to 18 and thereby help the national team by allowing more time for the national team to train together etc. Of course this never happened, and is never likely to, but to think about actually increasing the number of games seems sheer lunacy."

Reading

Chairman of the Supporters Trust At Reading (STAR) **Paula Martin** doesn't understand why the Premier League, rated the best in the world, is "scared" of their European counterparts but admits that if the 39th game is given the go-ahead she would "seriously consider" her position as a football fan.

The 39th Game: Premier League plays at imperialism

"If the Premier League had confidence in their 'product' they would not be scared of other European leagues. The alternative Super League does have some credibility and many fans of teams other than the 'big four' would welcome their removal as it would create a much fairer competition.

"I would not travel to any such games but I know of several fans who do not miss a single game and they would probably have to admit defeat and miss a league game. It is the fact that it would be a league game that is so damaging.

"I think that a fair number of fans would turn their back on the Premier League, as a newcomer to the top flight there are many Reading fans already disillusioned by the money game that is the Premier League and this would most definitely be a last straw to turn them to local non-league football.

"Whilst acknowledging evolution, it is the very thought that this is only the first step that is most worrying both in terms of abandoning the home and away only principle and also in removing the league from its community roots. Playing abroad is no problem, but playing a league game is so I would support another competitive competition with no hesitation."

And Paula's admission is shared amongst most of the football community. The Premier League was designed to bring the best players from around the world to these shores, not so we could take our game around the world.

Sunderland

Sunderland fan **Tony Ratton**, who is a season ticket holder at the Stadium of Light and takes his 11-year-old son to matches, said the plan is just a cash cow.

"I feel that the 39 game season plan is nonsense and hopefully it will not get past the planning stage. It's obviously very money driven and a cash cow. The fact that they are looking to seed the top teams says it all. What happens if say Bolton get drawn to play Wigan? What sort of interest is that going to generate? If any of the bottom six have to play the top six three times in a season how will they feel about this. Those three points could be the difference between staying up or returning to the Championship."

West Ham United

West Ham fan **Matthew Beeby**, from Slough, is another dead against the plan. He said:

"It's a nonsense idea dreamt up by money-hungry idiots, turning the league into nothing more than a travelling freak show, performing tricks for the highest bidder.

"It's hard to see what the advantages are to the common fan. The money paid to the clubs will never be filtered down through cheaper tickets prices. They might get a nice shiny new striker for the cash – but then so will every other club in the league, there's no financial advantage to it compare to the other clubs. The clubs might gain some extra fans in Bangalore, but the likelihood is that they will simply jump onto the bandwagon of the supposed big

four, leaving the other clubs as nothing more than the obliging bait to tempt in Manchester United's latest set of plastic fans."

Not all foreign Premier League fans are backing the scheme. West Ham fan **David Lewis**, who writes his own blog, ozhammers.com, on the happenings at Upton Park, believes that you can't take the electric atmosphere of the Premier League around the world.

He wrote:

"My view – BIG MISTAKE! The whole experience that is the EPL is not transportable and those who think it is are deluded. Any fan who has been to their home ground with the home fans to see their team play knows exactly what I mean. Anfield, Old Trafford, Goodison Park, Upton Park and even all the other second tier grounds have their own atmosphere and feeling. You simply cannot bring that with you when the teams tour. All the new stadia spend considerable effort to rebuild the elements that made their original ground so special. Some succeed and some don't but at the end of the day you just can't transplant the home fans.

"The objective here is financial and promotional. I think there are far better ways to achieve these objectives without damaging the real drawing power of the EPL.

"Somehow I think (hope) its back to the drawing board on this one!"

Wigan Athletic

Wigan Athletic supporter **Carl Miller** wrote on a Wigan footymad fans' forum:

"This would prove once and for all that the clubs and powers that be don't care about the fans. It's alright for United, Liverpool, etc, those with a global image, but not for Wigan. If they want to go, fire the top four off and tell them to get to their bloody G14. (It) would make the Premiership competitive and fair, without the glorybores from the top four, same old, same old, EVERY frickin year. It is going to implode and our game will end up in ruins. Why? Greed."

"As if taking the Premier League around the world wasn't bad enough the fact that they are even contemplating seeding the top clubs has been a real slap in the face for the fans, especially when it could have a huge say in determining the Premier League winners, European qualification and relegation.

One Wigan Athletic fan, **jg_wiganfc26**, wrote on a footymad forum saying it was:

"... a complete farce."

"If we were safe on the 38th Premiership game and then had to play, for instance, Manchester United, and then lost and got relegated, it would be a complete farce to the Premiership and has sent someone down by wanting to get more money by playing games across the world. Also, they spoke to the 20 Premiership clubs they say. What difference does that make? Who says the same 20 would be there when they do it?"

Bristol City

We also cast our net beyond the Premier League – to the clubs that might one day be part of it. **James Nicholls**, a foreign based Bristol City fan only sees three or so games a season these days but is convinced that the plan is designed to aid the big clubs and is simply wrong:

"I [don't think any other country will attempt it] as Fifa are against it, if they gave the green light then I think a number of countries would consider it, but it would only be the teams who have enough "fan" potential... i.e. the big clubs

"As usual you have clubs going into administration for what is the equivalent of a months wages for some players in the Premiership which is not a problem as they get paid what the market dictates. It all boils down to a bit of wealth distribution coming down the leagues. These teams are part of the community, employ any number of people, provide entertainment and offer up potential future international players for the home countries- you could go on and on but I do not think many of the big clubs look past their own nose and its profit for today."

Leeds United

Georgina Jane Petty is a die-hard Leeds fan, who is currently boycotting Elland Road in protest at Ken Bates "hitting the fans in the pocket" and feels that the plan is designed to aid the biggest clubs:

"...to increase their marketability, make the likes of Ronaldo and Rooney even more rich and alienate even more fans from the game. Whatever happened to it being a "grassroots" sport! We're practically uprooting and bulldozing all that is exciting, compelling and endearing about our English game...

"... considering international managers and some players are complaining that there's too many games, it's just going to hamper the international scene and the progress of the Premiership in general. We must be doing something right if so many foreigners want to take a chance on the Premiership when they could've gone to Serie A or La Liga. If it aint broke why fix it comes to mind....

"If football is purely about business, which to the cynic, maybe its leaning that way, it would be a way of increasing revenue, I'm just not sure the supporters of Everton and Fulham with small-ish squads would be enamoured with a huge trip as the likes of Man U and Chelsea who would only increase their monopolies and their players are used to extravagant oversees PR stunts anyway...

"[For the lower leagues] the gap in wealth, talent and scouting pools gets wider and the chance of becoming more predictable like the Scottish Premier League, will sadly increase!

"I have been to some fantastic stadiums and some very grotty stadiums in this country, but most of them have all had one appealing factor, whether it be hail, rain or shine, the atmosphere has usually been exciting, amusing, intriguing, inspiring, one of *my most favourite games was Leeds vs Lokomotiv Moscow and it THREW it down with hailstones, I was wearing my Leeds shirt and thin denim jeans I got totally soaked but I didn't care. It was hilarious, thrilling, I think having a game abroad kills the spontaneity and blood and guts aspect of English football that we're trying to preserve."*

West Bromwich Albion

Final word to a Baggies fan, who will be in the Premier League in 2008/9, do you want to guess which way **Jon Newsome** leans?

"The 39th game proposals are daft. 20 teams in a league give 38 games - given teams play each other home and away - a fair and reasonable system. Who decides which team you will play in the 39th game? Your league position perhaps? I can see them flocking in to watch Derby vs Bolton in New York!

"The marketing and money people are turning the heads of officials who feel they have to come up with something to justify their existence. It's rubbish.

"Incidentally, I support West Bromwich Albion. Now there's a team that will bring them flocking in in Bejing!"

Chapter 8: From European League To World League?

By Hugh Larkin

> *"There will be a super professional football league like American Football, which will attract millions of viewers."*

Silvio Berlusconi 1998 in World Soccer.

When the Premier League announced their plan to take extra games around the world, it's fair to say that the proposal received a lukewarm response in many quarters- not least FIFA and Sepp Blatter.

Richard Scudamore stuck to his guns as the negative responses mounted and his argument that this proposal will become accepted by enough people eventually has more merit than is obvious at first glance.

The Chief Executive's argument turns on his point that innovations often draw negative comment when first mooted only to be welcomed as key features of the global game at some point in the future. In fact, Scudamore is actually part of a long tradition

The 39th Game: Premier League plays at imperialism

***

Back in 1888- even before the Football League had kicked into life - an enterprising promoter enticed West Bromwich Albion, then the FA Cup holders in England, to play Scottish Cup winners Renton in a game titled 'The Championship of the World'.

Even in Victorian times the idea of cross-border competition was with us, although it wasn't to be British clubs that carried the idea forward. Once Europe has caught on to the idea of organised football, the close proximity of several countries brought the idea of regular cross-border competition to the fore.

Long before the European Cup came on the scene, top club sides in Central Europe were competing for the Mitropa Cup that began way back in 1927. At the time - and much to the chagrin of British Associations - Central European teams were leading the way in technique and organisation.

British teams were never going to be involved but the competition kicked off with club sides from countries like Czechoslovakia, Austria, Hungary and Italy and could justly be called the peak of club football in the Pre-war era. After WW2 its status had declined although it was revived as the Zentropa Cup

One of the ironies of the Premier League position is that the English FA and its acolytes were long seen as the main opponents of cross-border club competition.

The Mitropa ideal demonstrated that some administrators and club officials were thinking outside the box well over 70 years ago and that the concept of European Super League was current even in the 1920s.

In 1955 there came the launch of the European Cup, though characteristically the English FA refused to allow champions Chelsea to take part. Hibernian did join the new venture on behalf of Scotland though and soon the idea of competition for national champions of Europe became widely accepted and wildly popular.

Alongside the senior European Cup though, there was what is now a little known junior competition that has far more importance in retrospect than it received at the time.

The Inter-Cities Fairs Cup commenced in 1956 and the original concept would be familiar to the movers and shakers in the modern game. This was a competition conceived with a business outcome in mind and explicitly designed to bring major cities into the mix.

Entry to the Fairs Cup was not based on domestic league position - the aim was to create a series of matches between teams from European cities that hosted major trade fairs. Successful provincial clubs need not apply. The initial competition brought together teams from London, Barcelona, Copenhagen, Leipzig, Birmingham, Frankfurt, Zagreb and Vienna,

Unfortunately it proved a nightmare to organise because the administrators chose a group system to increase the number of matches (sound familiar?) and cities like London were represented by one team. The competition had a one city, one team rule for its first few years.

London was a composite eleven made up of players from 6-7 capital sides including Brentford. The first competition took over two years to complete and some sides withdrew along the way. In the next two renewals teams like Barcelona played in both the European Cup and the Fairs Cup because there was little co-ordination at the time.

Though all European football would eventually come under UEFA, in the early days the Fairs Cup operated effectively as a rival to the European Cup. The fact that the latter prize brought together all the national champions won it greater recognition from fans.

By 1962 the organisers of the Fairs Cup had conceded pre-eminence to the Champions Cup and the trophy carved out a different niche as a competition for teams finishing highly placed in the domestic leagues. The name change to the UEFA Cup in 1971 removed the anachronistic title.

The concepts implicit in the Fairs Cup never totally went way though. European club football proved to be runaway success and when the time proved to be ripe, the 'Super League' ideal would come back to the fore.

***

From 1955 to 1992 the European Cup grew to be the premier trophy on the Continent and the pinnacle of achievement for club teams. In that period the format remained the same- a two leg knockout system for all the national champions of UEFA's member associations.

Over more than three decades changes were taking place in the wider world of sports - and Europe in general - that raised a groundswell of opinion among some clubs to alter the traditional format of the Champion's Cup.

The most significant of these was growth of television broadcasting. Strange as it may seem to viewers early in the 21st Century, their counterparts in the 1970s in Britain would get to watch only one live domestic club match per year- the FA Cup Final.

Even the Football League's own showpiece Cup Final would only be shown as highlights on Sunday because of the possible effect televising the game live would have on League attendances- this was a time when every game kicked off at 3pm on Saturdays.

From the United States though, administrators and club directors could see a different vision of the relationship between television and sport and it was one that delivered riches to the participants.

American Football (and other US sports) worked hand in glove with television to deliver a product for the armchair viewers which delivered massive revenues in sponsorship and advertising. The game had to be altered in subtle and not so subtle ways to accommodate TV- more cameras, changed kick off times etc but overall the symbiosis produced money and lots of it.

The expansion of major US sports like Gridiron and Ice Hockey (the NHL once had just 6 clubs) also offered a model for the way a competition could be run across a whole Continent, albeit one made up of just two nations.

As domestic football in the UK became increasingly sterile in the 1970s the proponents of European leagues made their voices heard again but the effects of the 1973 Oil Crisis put a dampener on ideas that involved more long distance travel.

By the early 1990s though, the European Super League was a live debate again. Football had become a richer game from the development of partnerships with television and the whole concept of 'Europe' had been boosted by moves toward political integration.

The future of satellite broadcasting opened up the prospect of a massive choice of channels, many of which might want to show even more football-based content. Many key decision-makers in European football had come to the conclusion that the game just didn't have enough 'product' to showcase.

The desire to get more top level games for television's new demands coincided with the self-interest of some of Europe's leading clubs who chafed at the restriction that only one team could enter the premier competition. In addition, the elite clubs were unhappy at the vagaries of knockout football.

Political changes in Europe provided clubs from Europe's biggest leagues- Western European ones- with the opportunity to force through their favoured alterations to the club structure.

The collapse of the Communist regimes and economies in Eastern Europe cut away the power of the leading clubs from that region as the German, Italian and Spanish leagues lured away the best talent from behind what had been the 'Iron Curtain'.

The East European Football Associations lost confidence and power among the turmoil and were unable to defend the status quo of 'one team, one nation' that had been at the heart of the Champions' Cup from the start.

Broadcasters made it clear that they wouldn't pay the same the same shilling to cover matches with teams shorn of their key players, or treat games involving smaller national champions with the same effort.

By 1992 UEFA had begun to realise the inevitability of acceding to some of the demands of the leading clubs allied as they were with the needs of the new media. There was an implicit threat from the non-terrestrial companies that they may fund their own competitions if some of their needs weren't met.

In 1991/92 instead of quarter-finals the last eight sides went onto two leagues, thus delivering 6 more guaranteed matches to the eight teams. From there it was a steady development to increase the league element and to invite more than one team to enter from Europe's most powerful countries.

By the mid-90's the Champion's Cup had become a Champion's League and certain clubs were returning to the competition every year. The European Super League appeared to be finally about to become a reality.

***

1998 was the year when the European Super League appeared inevitable and one man drove the plans above all others. Silvio Berlusconi, the television magnate and new owner of AC Milan was candid about his vision for the European game.

The future Prime Minister of Italy gave interviews in which he argued for a Europe wide League where there would be game every Friday night between two of the biggest clubs on the Continent, which would be watched the length of Europe - Iceland to Greece.

The tone of his various pronouncements gave the impression that the creation of the Super League was simply inevitable and during 1998 there is no doubt that some of Europe's elite clubs gathered for serious discussion on the topic.

A number of pivotal meetings took place but the projected Super League never came about. In 2000 14 of Europe's elite teams formed the G-14 organisation to represent their views to UEFA and FIFA but the Super League breakaway never occurred.

In 1998 the moment appeared to have arrived but the clubs did not take the final step and there were a number of reasons- one of them was the overbearing personality of Berlusconi who appropriated the idea but his impartiality as both club owner and TV magnate may have undermined his case.

The key factor is that beyond a certain point the G-14 clubs found that there were limits to their commonality of interest. The crucial question has always been - which clubs will make up the new competition?

While the likes of Milan, Real Madrid and Barcelona can always be viewed as certain invitees a number of other sides could have no such certainty. England provides a good example with Manchester United, Arsenal and Liverpool all members of the G-14.

On European performance Liverpool are by far the senior club but on revenue Manchester United top the pile. Could all three - not to mention Chelsea - be certain of an invite?

A second, related factor has been the very success of the UEFA Champions League. The product delivers exactly what European broadcasters and sponsors want- high profile matches involving the Continent's elite. Yet there has also been evidence that there is a limit to the amount of League competition Europe's viewers will tolerate.

UEFA removed the second group stage of the competition because of concerns that the public were being turned off by so many matches required before the knockout stages. There were rumblings from the G-14 group but the evidence on viewing figures undercut their case.

The surprise factor is that the Champions League and domestic tournaments have found a way to co-exist - at least for the elite. The lucrative rewards earned in Europe have allowed the major clubs to bolster their positions domestically; they carry bigger squads and can buy up the available talent from challengers.

The point has been reached where some clubs can put out two selections in a week in different competitions. For Manchester United. Arsenal and others the annual return to the Champions league has been factored into their business model.

To remain in their domestic leagues avoids the greatest leap into the unknown that the Super League would represent- a diminished chance to win things. Supporters of the elite clubs are more than ever gorged on winning trophies which begs the question of how they (and sponsors) would react to coming bottom of a Super League.

For the moment, enough teams have decided that they do well enough out of the Champions League format to leave it alone. In February 2008 G-14 even disbanded, an indication of the victory won by the members since the early 90s.

***

The 39th Game: Premier League plays at imperialism

Is it unconnected that the Premier League plan has been promoted at the time when G-14 disbands? It's highly unlikely. The initiative of the Premier League shows why the European Super League is no longer the only game in town.

For decades Europe has been the centre of world football but the last decade has the Continent severely challenged for its pre-eminence. The venues that the Premier League hoped to take their 39th Step games to, pinpoints the reality - North America and Asia with a nod toward Australia.

Asia has already become the economic powerhouse in the game of cricket and Far Eastern investment has started to make an impact on the Premiership; American money is pouring into several English teams and Russian cash also talks.

Many of the elite European clubs already spend a fair amount of time travelling around the globe playing friendlies and mini-tournaments in Asia, the Middle East and North America.

Football has always been a game centred on Europe and South America but the global game has made massive strides in the past three decades. Africa now provides a high proportion of the game's top performers but Asia and the Middle East are catching up rapidly.

There is now a large fan base in Asia developed through the global marketing and television exposure, so much so that cities like Hong Kong, Shanghai and Dubai were the natural targets of the Premier League's international round. North America has always been a holy grail for football administrators and this proposal would be one more attempt to crack that market.

Since the 1920s the European Super League has been the dominant vision of those who favour a supra-national league competition as the ultimate destiny for football but now the European only concept could be seriously challenged.

Once a European Super League could be discussed as an exotic, intoxicating idea but key features have been with us for the past 15 years. What the visionaries didn't predict was the clubs' ability to maintain a stranglehold on domestic competition at the same time, or the enduring tribalism that has halted any plans to create city super teams.

The 'newer' continents are actually in a position to deliver far more effectively on a 'franchise' system and of course Asia and North America have already successfully launched their own versions of the Champions League.

If any competition is ever going to be formed on the basis of one-club franchises in major conurbations, a global blueprint is now a far more likely way forward, given that many of the European elite clubs have achieved huge commercial success in the present structure.

The chances of Europe's elite sides agreeing on mergers in cities like London and Milan is virtually nil, so looking beyond the confines of Europe looks like a proposition worth exploring.

Of all the senior European leagues the Premier is the one positioned to be a pathfinder because of the influx of non-European investment coming to its clubs. Increasingly the English sides appear to be out of step with their counterparts in Spain and Italy where there is resistance to outside cash and influence.

The 39th Game: Premier League plays at imperialism

***

There is a cautionary note for any Premier League executive with visions of global dominance. If the League and its member clubs did decide to go down the route of effectively setting up globally, the rest of Europe would hardly take it lying down.

G-14 could easily be revived under another name with English clubs excluded and there would be the basis for taking forward a European blueprint again, or indeed a global product.

In this admittedly unlikely scenario, G-14 clubs that have been a thorn in the side of UEFA and FIFA could suddenly be firmly in the establishment camp.

Another possibility is that with English sides out on a limb the rest of Europe would fall behind FIFA and UEFA if those bodies agreed an international ban for players serving in the global Premiership. Though there has been a tendency to downplay international soccer over the past decade it remains the pinnacle of a most player's careers.

Undoubtedly negotiation would ensue before any clear decision was reached but the rest of the world does have mechanisms to fight back if the Premier League tries to take too big a slice of the game's pie.

G-14 does actually have successor- the European Club Association. This is a far more democratic body bringing together 103 members from 53 countries. Premiership teams are involved in it of course and it may be a welcome forum in which to take soundings about how other clubs feel about the Premier League's plans.

UEFA is far more comfortable with the ECA as a body – and the European Club's Forum which has also been disbanded. The ECA is a logical response to the realities of the Champions League.

Given that most of Europe's elite clubs have discovered that the currently constituted competition is of greater benefit to them than a chimerical European Super League (for reasons outlined above), it made sense to reconnect with what could be termed the 'middle ranking' outfits.

Many of these are champions in their own countries and have found that regular participation in the Champions League has enabled them to establish dominance in their domestic competitions, even if they don't reach the last 16 very often. Among these sides there is little appetite for any more than tinkering with the system.

The ECA is a very new body and it remains to be seen if it can be effective as G-14 was on certain issues. 103 members is unwieldy but certain clubs can be expected to take the lead.

The expanded membership certainly makes key individuals like Michel Platini more comfortable about dialogue than with the avowedly elitist G14. ECA will be a powerful voice in soccer and could channel some sharp opinions to its English member clubs.

***

Despite the chorus of disapproval from the likes of FIFA, UEFA and the Asian Confederation, the Premier League may well be swimming with the global tide.

The 39th Game: Premier League plays at imperialism

There are areas of the world where fans and more critically owners/organisers, have an appetite for top quality competitive football, beyond just watching in television. Friendly tours can only assuage some of this demand and the Premier League will continue to forge links across the globe.

The rest of Europe's top clubs can be expected to keep a careful eye on the plans- the 39th game alone is probably not too much of threat to their interests but if it is conduit to ever more riches flowing to English sides, some retaliatory action or competition must take place. For the moment though, the ECA clubs will hold a watching brief and let FIFA, UEFA and National Associations fight their corner.

As with most matters in the world today, the attitude of the media will be the key. The happenings in Indian cricket at the moment are instructive. The appearance of a breakaway one day league prompted the authorities to create their own to run alongside.

Both competitions have not been short of sponsors or media companies willing to bid big money to carry the coverage. Certain broadcasters have their exclusive contacts with the game's authorities but there are plenty of others waiting to pick up a slice of the action by hosting rival competitions.

If television can be persuaded to come on board and enough promoters can be found to stage and underwrite the matches, the international round may yet be a reality- and when that happens it will spark a debate not about the formation of European Super League but a truly global one.

Chapter 9: What about the rest of us?

By Paul Grech

> "To promote and encourage local community and fan ownership of football clubs."

Taken from the Dons Trust (owners of AFC Wimbledon) organisation aims document

Fate has been harsh on Sheffield Wednesday. When Dave Richards was asked to vote for the formation of a breakaway league on 17 July 1991, the prospects for his club looked good. After some years in the Second Division, Wednesday had established themselves in the top flight finishing third at the end of the 1991-92 season and winning the League Cup in 1991. The money that the new television deals were promising them was to help them challenge the big five and place them permanently as one of the country's leading sides.

That, at least, was the theory and the reason why Wednesday voted for the formation of the Premier League just as everyone else. It was the sensible option, particularly if you owned the club and stood to gain handsomely from the new deals.

Looking at Wednesday today, however, and the feeling is that the turkeys voted for Christmas. Struggling in the Championship and heavily in debt, they're unlikely to make it back to the top flight any time soon. Much more likely is another relegation to Division One and the sale of any promising players that come through.

What happened at Wednesday is indeed eye opening. The new deals put pressure on the club not to improve but rather to ensure that they stayed in the Premier League. Huge money was spent on Wim Jonk (£2.5 million), Gilles De Bilde (£3 million), Andy Booth (£2.7 million) and Gerald Sibon (£2 million) yet none of them paid off. Rather than progressing as had been prospected, Sheffield Wednesday were relegated at the end of the 1999-2000 season.

And that was just the start of their problems. In its gamble to stay in the Premier League the club had overspent, running up debts of £16 million. They were also lumbered with a squad of players on Premier League wages yet clearly incapable of getting them back to the top flight. With none of the players willing to leave for a lower wage, Wednesday were stuck with them as the financial hole in which they had dug themselves got bigger and bigger.

It is a financial problem that burdens them to this day and one that should serve as a lesson to any club willing to go on the same route.

But, of course, that hasn't happened. Instead the list of clubs to have gambled in the dream of cashing in on the Premier League's big money continues to grow. Leeds United have gone a similar way although they've done so more spectacularly and dramatically than anyone else. Yet they aren't the only ones.

Scour through the lower league tables and you're bound to spot others who are either still reeling or else trying to recover from their excesses. The St. Mary's Stadium at Southampton and the Ricoh Arena at Coventry are two monuments to such crushed dreams. For both clubs, moving to new stadiums had become a necessity yet what both failed to plan for is that they would have to pay for them with the revenues available to Championship clubs.

There is also Nottingham Forest, twice winners of the European Cup in an era when this meant being the top club in Europe rather than a huge windfall of revenue. Forest is now struggling to make it back into the Championship. They too overspent, first in a bid to stay in the Premier League and then in an attempt to get back there.

By 2003, they looked to have come out of it and a team brimming with young talent looked set to give them what money had failed to. The club's financial past, however, soon sucked that dream away as one by one the players were sold. Jermaine Jenas, Andy Reid and Michael Dawson should have taken Forest back into the Premier League but they were never given the opportunity.

***

Yet, given the opportunity, it is a safe bet that many of those clubs would do the same. It is not an idle statement but merely one based on clubs' willingness to go down the same route. Everyone claims to have learned from others' mistakes but then go on to repeat them. Cardiff and the mess they've got themselves into as they tried to win promotion is ample proof of that.

The truth is that the financial jackpot if the gamble pays off is huge. Money was at the basis of the formation of the Premier League and remains the biggest incentive for clubs eager to make it there, so big an incentive that many risk their club's own existence.

Reactions of surprise and shock might have greeted the Premier League's announcement of holding another game overseas but, in reality, it is something that should have been expected out of a body where the generation of revenue seems to be the only objective. Holding games overseas isn't being done for the improvement of the English game but rather to make the members of this exclusive club richer.

What is ironic for clubs like Sheffield Wednesday who voted for the Premier League is that they were knowingly agreeing that any financial wealth created by the new league would be kept exclusively within that same league. It seemed a good decision for them when they were on the other side on the fence, much less now.

At least the Premier League is finally contributing to the lower divisions. Not through any spirit of generosity but simply to quell threats of potential investigation by the European Union and, even so, the amounts being handed out are simply a fraction of what is generated.

But it isn't all bad. At least, certain doomsday scenarios that were put about upon the formation of the Premier League haven't materialised.

One of the biggest fears when the rights for top flight games were first sold to Sky was that this would kill off small clubs. The argument was that an ever decreasing number of fans would continue following their local side with the majority opting for the glamour of supporting the big teams, even if exclusively from the television.

Deprived of gate money, for many the only real source of income, clubs would simply be starved out of existence.

Not only have such fears never come to be but the opposite has happened as an increasing number of clubs in the Conference are going full time to increase the number of professional clubs in England. Again, in some cases, there are shades of the greed that has threatened the existence of club higher up the league structure and for some this was simply a gamble too far by egomaniacal owners. Yet most clubs have managed to survive and prosper with this set up, proof perhaps of football's increasing appeal.

In this context, the Premier League's greed works in favour of smaller clubs. Priced out of watching the clubs they've supported for years, fans have two options: either resort to following games on television or else choosing a new club where they can get their weekly fix of live football. Of course, most people opt for the first option but there are still many who are succumbing to the lure of the second.

Holding games overseas is sure to alienate more fans than it will generate which should be good news for lower league clubs.

***

There is, however, another more specific reason that has really ensured the survival of a good number of clubs within the league structure: the local, hardcore element of fans, the same people that the Premier League seems to consider as disposable.

What started out as occasional instances of fans coming together to help save their club has today evolved into the highly organised and efficient Supporters Direct which provides focus for the fans of any club who want to form a Supporters Trust.

For the uninitiated a Trust is an independent, democratically-organised supporters' organisation that seeks to represent the views of the fans to the club and help promote communication from the club to the fans. All Trusts are formally-constituted legal bodies typically in the form of an Industrial and Provident Society.

In strictly legal terms, this means that all Trusts have to follow and uphold certain requirements such as being a not-for profit organisation, holding an Annual General Meeting and having their accounts examined by an independent, qualified auditor.

What Trusts provide in reality is a framework that allows fans to organise themselves and raise funds that enable them to get a say in the running of the club. Often this happens in times of crisis, where clubs need money to stay afloat and owners have little alternative to selling a share of the club to Trusts.

In some circumstances, however, the fans have been even more ambitious. Fans of Brentford, Notts County and Stockport County have gone the whole way and taken over their clubs. And, that's simply taking into consideration the clubs in the Football League.

Returning clubs to the community, something that was long held to be impossible, is becoming not only plausible but for many clubs the only option in order to stave off bankruptcy.

Yet the model isn't without its pitfalls. Raising funds consistently is one of them, as York City's supporters found out. When the fans raised around £200,000 in order to buy the club from John Batchelor in 2003, the dream was that this would usher a period of relative stability after half a decade of constant turmoil.

It didn't prove to be the case. They were relegated to the Conference by the end of the 2003-04 season and two years later the Trust's board informed members that unless significant funding could be secured, they would have to investigate the club's solvency. A deal proposing the sale of the majority ownership to JM Packaging was strongly recommended and eventually went through.

Fans will remain to be the life-blood of lower league clubs, their main source of revenue and the ones who will pull up their sleeves when there are any problems. Yet, apart from some exceptions, it is hard to envisage a situation where they can actually own the club.

***

There is another, much different route for fans to take ownership of their fate: by setting up their own club.

The Premiership's success has come at a price. It is impossible, for instance, to deny that the demographics of the match going public has changed with the working class that traditionally formed the bedrock of English support being replaced by those financially better off.

The plan to add a thirty-ninth game to the fixture list, which game would be played overseas confirmed just how detached English club have become with their roots.

So alienated have a group of Liverpool fans become that they've decided to look for an alternative to the current situation, that of forming their own club.

February 2008 saw the official launching of AFC Liverpool Grassroots, which, according to their promotional literature, is aimed at "those Liverpool fans who have been priced out of watching Premier League games."

Alun Parry, the man who came up with the whole idea, counts himself among such fans.

"The overriding driver is that there is a genuine affordability issue when it comes to Premier League matches."

The 37 year-old goes on to explain:

"They're extremely expensive and there are many diehard Reds who simply can't afford to pay close to £40 week in week out to get to see a game.

"Those who have kids are even harder hit financially. I know one lad who gave up his own season ticket because he couldn't afford to take his son to the game too, and felt mean leaving his football mad boy behind every Saturday to go to Anfield himself.

The 39th Game: Premier League plays at imperialism

"That's not to have a pop at Liverpool FC. In fact, if you compare the pricing policy of all the Premiership clubs, Liverpool offers relatively good value and LFC has been far more sensitive than most to the needs of their local community.

"But that aside, the nature of Premier League football is that, even if our prices are kinder than others, they're still too expensive for massive amounts of Liverpool supporters. Many can't go at all, many others can only afford to go to a few games a year.

"What happens to those supporters is the question. To be able to provide a football club run by Liverpool fans means that they can come and support us with fellow Reds, wearing the same colours, sharing the terrace with the same community of Liverpool supporters, singing the same songs. Okay its not Liverpool itself, but it has a Liverpool FC identity, and it will hopefully bring many people back through the turnstiles. It's sad that many kids grow up primarily experiencing football as a TV show.

"For some, the solution has been that of following another club lower down the league structure. Yet this is not something that is likely to appeal to most fans.

"For most Liverpool fans, we have always focused on LFC and it's doubtful if we could just invent support for another club out of thin air. If I went to watch another team plucked out of thin air like that, I'd enjoy it because I enjoy watching football, but I wouldn't enjoy it on the level that a supporter would.

"The thing that is unique about AFC Liverpool is the fact that it exists for the community of Liverpool supporters, and so the club will have an identity that people can hook into and so genuinely care about the result.

"If you currently have an affinity with Tranmere or Formby or Marine or Prescot Cables or Bootle FC or Southport or any of the other fine teams in Merseyside then yes go along and support them.

"But we know that most Liverpool supporters don't have that reason to support another team, and fandom cannot simply be invented as we all know. So many football fans are currently spending Saturday afternoons away from football. AFC Liverpool is a reason for them to come back, and be part of a team they have a genuine reason to support."

Agree or not with AFC Liverpool, it is undeniably that there is more than a fair share of truth in Parry's arguments. Proof lies in the popularity of reserve team football, with Liverpool's home games regularly attracting figures in the thousands – there were more than 10,000 for the recent game with Manchester United - specifically because they offer fans the opportunity of watching their team without having to fork out half their pay.

There is also the question of values:

"There is great skill in the Premiership so top flight football does have its sparkle. But, as the Game 39 moneyfest showed, it's lost a lot of its soul in the chase for cash. I think Game 39 proved to everyone that the people running the game care more about money than they do about the integrity of the competition itself. Many supporters who can still afford to go the game nonetheless *miss the more traditional values of the game, and would enjoy going along to AFC Liverpool as well."*

Just how much greed has entrenched itself in the soul of the Premier League is shown by the growing number of foreign owned clubs, all bought because they're deemed a good investment that will generate money for the owners.

Liverpool is one such club, although Parry is at pains to stress that the formation of AFC Liverpool Grassroots is in no way a response to the controversial ownership of Tom Hicks and George Gillett.

"People tend to think this is a reaction to Hicks & Gillett in the way that FC United was seen as a reaction to Glazer, but its not. It's an unfortunate coincidence that Hicks and Gillett are about as people jump to the conclusion that it's all about them when it's not at all about them."

Whatever the perception, the idea has been welcomed.

"The feedback has been excellent,"

Parry confirms.

"There is a real buzz around the idea and people are very keen."

Given the resentment to the current owners, that was always likely to be the case yet feelings are likely to change were the club to change hands. That, however, isn't something that worries Parry.

"As I say this is not a response to the owners. The owners just happen to be there. I think in many ways it will be easier for us once the ownership issue is cleared up because people will realise that this is not a reaction to that, but is motivated by other issues and is a genuine idea in its own right.

"Whoever owns Liverpool Football Club over the next however many years, ticket prices will still be high enough to price many diehard Reds out of supporting the team in the way we could in my Dad's day.

"AFC Liverpool is primarily targeting those supporters, to be part of an LFC community, attending a real "in the flesh" football match, standing with the same fans, wearing the same colour scarves, and singing the same songs.

"No matter who owns LFC, the demands of the Premiership will still be pricing genuine Reds out of the game. The question is, where can they go to watch a football match that they care about? Where can they take their kids to be part of that community that I experienced as a lad going to the game? AFC Liverpool is the answer to that question - and that question remains, no matter who owns LFC."

What comes next is arguably the biggest challenge that the young club is yet to face.

The 39th Game: Premier League plays at imperialism

"Our next step is to allow people to put their money where their mouth is and make this a reality. The basis of the club is that it will be an Industrial & Provident Society which is the standard model for supporter owned clubs. We'll soon be inviting people to send us money which will then become your membership of the club.

"It is key to our acceptance into the league that we have that financial backing and money in the bank so we'll be making an announcement on how people can financially support the creation of the club, and in the process become a voting member of the club too."

For all of his positive talk, Parry is realistic enough to realist that:

"There are some who are suspicious that this is an anti-LFC thing"

Yet he isn't going to be discouraged by this. Calls have already gone out for anyone willing to either manage or play for the new club.

"I think those who talk to us and realise our motivations can see that it's anything but, and that everybody involved is passionate about Liverpool Football Club too."

The 39th Game: Premier League plays at imperialism

Chapter 10: The Greed League

By Colin Illingworth, Antony Melvin

"Greed, for lack of a better word, is good. Greed is right. Greed works. Greed clarifies, cuts through, and captures the essence of the evolutionary spirit. Greed, in all of its forms, greed for life, for money, for love, knowledge has marked the upward surge of mankind."

Gordon Gecko

English football fans have to put up with a lot of crap. When they follow their club in European competitions the chances are they will come home with a blood stained shirt and stitches, courtesy of the local constabulary. When they go to away grounds in this country they are often given the worst seats in the ground, constantly threatened by power crazed stewards to sit down or get thrown out, and pay more than the home fans on some occasions for the privilege. And even if you've followed your club everywhere for the whole season and you reach a cup final there's still a strong chance that you won't be able to get a ticket as they've set aside 30 per cent of the stadium for corporate guests. Not to mention the soaring ticket prices, the cost of refreshments in the ground, satellite subscriptions, merchandise and travel costs on top.

However, the English nation isn't one to cause a fuss and just gets on with it because they love the game so much. But Richard Scudamore's plan to take a Premier League game out of the country could be the straw that breaks the camel's back. Since he revealed that plans were afoot to take the English game around the world there has been a worldwide backlash.

The Football Supporters' Federation (FSF), the champion of English football fans, launched an online petition against the plan and received more than 4,000 signatures in less than 24 hours. FSF head of policy Steven Powell, an Arsenal fan, called on the fans to unite against the plans. He said:

"Yet again, those running our national game have displayed a complete disregard for the interests of those without whom there would be no show – the fans themselves. They've simply gone too far, and the time has arrived for football supporters to stand up and be counted."

English fans are some of the most passionate supporters in the world and are prepared to do anything they can to follow their club. You only have to look at the thousands of ticket-less Liverpool fans who descended on Athens for the Champions League final in 2007 desperate to say: "I was there". And there's no question that if this global idea was given the go-ahead that a section of the most hardcore fans would sacrifice everything in order to be there. But why should they? The Premier League is an English product and already has a worldwide appeal. Why take the game thousands of miles around the world for a match, which, if the seeding of the top five goes ahead, will ultimately give the big boys an unfair advantage?

Yes under the plans of Mr Scudamore, each Premier League club is expected to make an extra £5 million, but the big winners will be the likes of your Arsenals, Manchester United's and Liverpool's through merchandise, thus creating an even bigger gap between the big clubs and the rest.

The Premier League is already the most popular football league in the world. More than half a billion people in 202 countries tune in to watch the Premier League every week, and it's undoubtedly the richest in the world. The latest television deal in the UK alone netted the league £1.7 billion, and when you add in the income from the global market it equates to £2.7 billion – almost £45 million a year for each club over three years. Not to mention the multi-million pound kit and sponsorship deals. Yet while all this money is being pumped into the game the ordinary fans continue to be priced out of it. In October 2007, The Independent printed a list of the most expensive tickets for Premier League clubs.

1 Arsenal £94
2 Tottenham Hotspur £71
3 Chelsea £65
4 West Ham United £61
5 Newcastle United £60
6 Sunderland £55
7 Fulham £50

8 Birmingham City £48

9= Derby County £44

9= Manchester United £44

11= Portsmouth £41

11= Reading £41

13 Middlesbrough £40

14 Bolton Wanderers £39

15 Liverpool £36

16= Aston Villa £35

16= Blackburn Rovers £35

18 Everton £34

18 Manchester City £34

20 Wigan Athletic £25

In what sort of world are we living in when the team languishing at the foot of the Premiership, Derby County, charges fans the same price as that of the reigning champions, Manchester United? While United fans lap up the attacking flair from the likes of Rooney, Ronaldo and Tevez, Derby County fans are being subjected to poor football and defeat after defeat. But that is where the chairmen have us by the short and curlies. They know that no matter what happens on the pitch the fans will never give up on their team. They may go away for a while until things improve, but they will never swap allegiance for another club.

A recent poll by Virgin Money revealed that the average football fan in England will spend almost £100,000 in a lifetime supporting their club – enough to pay off the average mortgage! That is a phenomenal show of commitment from those who are the lifeblood of the game. But that isn't enough for the money-hungry chairman, who value corporate guests more highly than those in the stands. They now want to suck the cash out of the fans from around the world as well.

Is it reasonable that the richest league in Europe should get richer and more powerful when the fans are seemingly the last to benefit? If the riches that have been pouring into English football had been accompanied by some kind of ticket price freeze then perhaps the predatory owners who have been circling the English game in recent years would not by now have taken over the farm. If English football hadn't already demonstrated an ability to raise prices more aggressively in the last few years than at any time in its history then the idea that owners could buy in (often in hugely leveraged deals) and make money would have remained a dream.

Before the Premier League's formation in 1989, Michael Knighton negotiated the purchase of Manchester United for £20m; his business plan included debt and taking profit out of the club. His ideas were roundly ridiculed and his backers pulled out. The suspicion remained that football clubs could not generate enough cash to pay off debt and provide profit; the supporters were the primary income stream and they would only pay so much. The old adage that the only way to make a small fortune out of a football club was to start with a large fortune seemed to hold true.

If a cap had been placed on the supporter take at any time since the boom in television revenue took hold then a limit to the amount that clubs could screw out of their fans would be in place; but without it it seems likely that the average ticket price will rise above £50 by 2010 and with it will go any resemblance this sport ever had to a peoples' game.

Football ticket prices have always been compared to other types of entertainment, in the 1970s and 1980s a football match was considered (and priced) like a cinema ticket; by the 1990s a night at the theatre was the usual comparator (as if it is a choice!) but now I guess we are approaching 'a meal at a Michelin starred restaurant' once travel and expenses are taken into account. By the 2020s will each match be comparable to a 'family holiday' or 'a small car'?

The clubs that benefit most from this lopsided financial arrangement are the ones with the richest fans and the ones that stay in the top flight for longest. In a perverse way these are obviously related sets of people. Richer fans tend to favour the richer entertainment and better facilities on offer at the 'big' clubs, and the 'big' clubs tend to avoid relegation. Over time as a handful of teams have become the mainstays of the division they have got richer and in turn attracted richer fans; and the clubs have not been dumb enough to avoid the conclusion that richer fans can afford higher prices. As prices rise more and more of the kind of middle-class punter that, now, mostly fill Premier League grounds are taking the places of the noisy proletariat who kept the clubs alive during the desperate 1980s.

***

In an increasingly affluent world there are clear signs that other sports are also keen on globalisation. The American football game at Wembley will be followed by more attempts to spread the word. The Indian Premier League tournament has grabbed most of the best cricket players in the world in a few short months of trying – simply because the money was there. I would bet money now that there will be IPL games in England within two years. Globalisation is already here in many sports.

The net aim of all these changes to traditional sports is to enrich people's lives with entertainment or distraction in a world where national boundaries are getting less distinct. Increasingly it seems that sportsmen of all stripes are following the money even if it comes at the cost of the team or country that nurtured them. Nothing truly novel there, but the scale of the abandonment is growing.

Whether it is Stephen Ireland considering international retirement at the age of 21 (his grandmother will be spinning in her … oh, nearly forgot); the mass international cricket defection to the pyjama party on India or the Brazilians suddenly popping up as European international footballers across Europe the sense of identity is being lost. Sportsmen are chasing money as recompense for a short career, and as a result globalisation is coming in one form or another to every significant sport. Golf is already there, as is tennis, cricket is arguably following and football cannot avoid the issue.

The losers will be those people who prize their 'tribe' (be it team, region, country, religion, race, football team or whatever) above mere fiscal concerns. In the drive for the global buck money will win.

And so, of course, the major winners will be the money men, attracted to the game by safe returns they can only be chortling into the Moet at just how much potential for financial reward exists in international sport.

And every year the rich will get richer as a result; the Greed League is here and is there anything that can stop it?

Chapter 11: Premier League 2020

By Paul Meadows

"The impact on the national game - one-sided football, a tediously predictable league, absurdly paid stars, a sleazy underworld of agents, increasingly cynical and stagnating crowds, a weakened national side and the growing covert campaign to create a closed shop to protect the interests of owners which will freeze the league's membership for all time - is clear."

Will Hutton

One of the most common dilemmas any football fan faces towards the end of each campaign is whether or not to renew their season ticket. Family commitments, work patterns, saving responsibilities and other issues can all come into play when April turns to May. But the biggest considerations are general disillusionment with your team and the cost of your ticket.

If you're getting up at 6 o'clock every morning and have already put in a three hour shift by the time your heroes have even thought about starting up their BMW seven series, it's not too much to expect them to show a bit of passion when they pull on your club's jersey every week. But if they give the impression they'd rather be somewhere else when the first whistle blows, then why should you fork out £30+ every other week?

Even fans of the more successful clubs have it hard. It's all very well watching your team bring in another expensive foreigner from the cream of Europe and then celebrating another trophy success every other season, but with such glory comes increased ticket prices and inevitably there will be a time when you will be priced out and some Johnny-Come-Lately will come along and take your place. In a way, it's almost as if your teams' success results in personal punishment to you.

I know of a Manchester United fan who had been watching his team before his age hit double figures. Towards the end of the 2006/07 season, his nerves were shot to pieces. It was one of the most exciting times in United's history, with the Premiership title in their grasp, a place in the FA Cup final against Chelsea already assured and a scintillating UEFA Champions semi-final first leg win over AC Milan already in the bag.

But rather than look forward to a possible repeat of the incredible 1999 Treble success, much of his thoughts were on his finances. Things had changed over the past eight years; he couldn't just use all his cash to feed his football addiction, he had a family to support now, a mortgage to pay. So instead of looking forward to a climatic campaign, he was worrying about the cost of his next season ticket which had just risen 12%, a trip to the new Wembley Stadium, and the possible logistical nightmare of getting to Athens.

This wasn't what he had bought into when he fell in love with football as a 5-year-old child, sat on his dad's lap watching Bryan

Robson's brace help sink Brighton & Hove Albion at Wembley. But this is what football had become since the mid-nineties, and more and more traditional working-class fans were bailing out, to be replaced with pinstriped businessmen and the prawn sandwich brigade. Gone are the days you could meet your friends a couple of hours before the game and stand together on the terraces; you can no longer plan your life around weekly 3pm kick-off times; and affordability is an increasing danger for the majority.

But this is the Premier League Monster which was born in August 1992, with two-hour previews before the big match on Sky Sports, which would then be followed with, would you believe, another match on a Monday night, complete with pre-match fireworks and half-time cheerleaders. Soon, there would be football on every night of the week. And if there was a gap to fill on a Saturday morning, just tell those zany Newcastle United fans to travel 300-odd miles to Portsmouth for a 12.45 kick-off.

Back in the pre-Premier League era news of a live televised game would break weeks ahead of the fixture. We'd all count down the days before the game, even if it involved two teams we had no affinity for. And then the following day the whole workplace would be talking about the game whilst school playgrounds would be full of kids trying to re-enact what they had witnessed. Ask anyone now if they saw the game at the weekend, and the chances are they will misinterpret your Villarreal v Getafe clash for a game from the French second division, or maybe a Nigerian Under-21 international they caught on Eurosport.

The game is now unrecognisable to the one many of us grew up watching. The chances of finding Frank Lampard making his way to

Stamford Bridge on the tube are as likely as a British tennis player collecting his third successive Wimbledon title. When Ian Wright signed one of his last contracts with Arsenal, he wasn't interested in what the details entailed and instead simply asked for a pen; such a repeat these days would be enough to send the average agent to an early grave.

Now many players have as many houses as they do fingers and buy cars as naturally as you and I may nip down to the local Spar to pick up a loaf of bread or a pint of semi-skimmed. One current Premier League player who is set to be out of contract with his club in the summer of 2008 has recently rejected an offer of £60,000-per-week to stay believing he is worth more, although he accepts he isn't a regular first team pick. So although he may only consider himself a substitute, he wants more money for being so. This same player, incidentally, has a cash machine in his mansion to save him mixing with us folk, although he must surely realise he has to leave his house to spend the cash?

But if this is the way our football is in the year 2008, how will it be in twelve years time? Will the Premier League bubble have burst once and for all to restore some sort of normality to our national game, or will the current obsession with money sweeping through top-level football simply be replaced with a new level of greed, with tickets evading all but the filthy-rich and players earning even more for doing even less?

***

The 39th Game: Premier League plays at imperialism

By the time the 2020/21 season begins the Premier League will be celebrating its 28th year. In the fifteen seasons since its inception there have been just four winners - United, Blackburn Rovers, Arsenal and Chelsea. In the first 28 seasons of the old Football League, there were eleven winners, including clubs such as Preston North End, West Bromwich Albion and The Wednesday. It is hard, if not impossible, to imagine another seven teams winning the Premier League in its current climate in the next fifty years, let alone from now until 2020.

Of the four winners of the Premier League to date, with the exception of the Ewood Park club the other three, together with Liverpool, have been dubbed the Big Four and are expected to dominate the game for years to come. Indeed, it is seen as a huge achievement if a team, like Everton did in 2005, has the temerity to gatecrash this quartet and finish in fourth place. Even bookmakers now open a market every season so you can bet on the Premier League winner 'without the Big Four'.

It is already widely accepted that there are divisions within a division in England's top flight. You have the aforementioned Big Four, who all consider anything other than winning the Premier League as a disappointment. Then the likes of Aston Villa, Everton, Manchester City, Newcastle and Tottenham Hotspur, who aim for a top-six place. This results in Uefa Cup qualification and with it regular Thursday night football and usually hollow hopes of bidding for a UEFA Champions League place the following season.

Then there are the Middlesbrough's, Portsmouth's and West Ham United's who, currently, plod along in mid-table. For these teams being in the Premier League seems to be their main ambition every season, and only when they reach that magical 40-point mark do they even dare to take stock. And then there are the teams who's sole ambition is to avoid relegation, so they can milk the big league cash cow for another twelve months: Bolton Wanderers, Fulham and Wigan Athletic, for example. They celebrate avoiding relegation in much the same way the champions celebrate winning the league.

So perhaps by 2020/21, these divisions within a division will no longer be assumed, but real. If you win promotion to the Premier League and fulfil the necessary criteria (stadium, history, finances, wow-ability) to join the big guns, it is on the understanding that the highest you can possibly finish is 15th. And if you manage that, then the following season you will replace the team who finished 14th and be given the green light to fight for mid-table mediocrity. And so it goes: the ninth place team will replace the eighth place team so they can challenge for fifth spot next term. But, of course, the fifth place team will only be invited - dared - to enter the top four when they have finished fifth for five seasons on the bounce (and only if a Big Four club have finished fourth for the same period of time).

For any current Championship side thinking it is hard enough to gain promotion to the Premier League nowadays, it could be even harder in the future. With the richest clubs already cemented in the top-flight, the Championship may offer just one promotion place – and finishing top of the league may not even guarantee this, as the winners face a two-legged play-off with the Premier League's bottom club in order to claim their place amongst the top clubs in the country.

Further down the pyramid, and League One remains the same albeit with just one automatic promotion place and another to be decided via the play-off system. League Two, however, has been split into two divisions – League Two North and League Two South. The winners of each travel to Wembley Stadium for a play-off, the winner of which gains entry to League One. So any club who gains promotion from the Conference to League Two, their gradual climb to the Premier League involves: winning their regional League Two division; winning the League Two play-off; winning League One; winning the Championship; and finally winning the Premier League play-off. And then only if they fill the aforementioned criteria regarding stadium capacity, history, finance etc.

Easy, eh...?

In 2020, being a member of the Big Four not only gives you the right to fight for the Premier League title, but it also gives you certain privileges. For example, whilst the teams outside of the elite must make up their 39-game domestic season with fixtures against the other 15 clubs, the Big Four must play each other six times a season: three games at home and three games away. From this little league, the top team plays the fourth placed team and the second team is paired with the third placed side for one final encounter at a neutral venue outside of Europe. To make up their 39-game fixture list, the Big Four are invited to select ten other teams who they will play home and away.

Other benefits for the Big Four in 2020 include the 48-hour venue change, of which there are two a season. This allows the elite to be able to change the venue of one of their home fixtures against a non Big Four club to a more exotic location at short notice. Although this may prove impossible for fans to make arrangements to attend the game, especially if the chosen game falls on a work night, they are reminded that the small-print in each Premier League ticket clearly outlines a strictly no-refund policy.

There is also the Big Four shopping window, which comes along in the first week of every month and allows them to take one player from each of the remaining sixteen Premier League clubs. There is no negotiating for the price of the fee. The Big Four club simply makes their offer to the Premier League board, and they will decide if the particular player has been valued correctly. But not wanting to upset the big boys of the league, initial offers are rarely considered insufficient.

And also, shock of all shocks, should one of the Big Four lose against one of the inferior teams in the league, they are entitled to submit a written appeal about the result within 24 hours. So, for instance, were Arsenal to dominate a game against, say, Birmingham City at the Emirates Stadium, but then lose to a late goal, they can appeal that the result was unjust and the points could be reversed. There is, naturally, no right of appeal for any clubs outside the Big Four.

As for the FA Cup, all teams outside of the Big Four will compete on a knockout basis until a winner is determined. This winner will then be drawn against a member of the Big Four, and the winner of this tie will join the three remaining members of the Big Four in the semi-finals. The League Cup, though, represents a great chance of silverware as there is no Big Four representation, although the rewards are limited since the termination of the Uefa Cup, which has made way for the UEFA Champion Super League (UCSL). The

UCSL is held every June/July in one country. 24 clubs (four each from England, Italy and Spain, and twelve others from various European nations) are split into four groups, the top two of which enter the knockout stages until a winner finally emerges.

This has rather taken the place of international football, which is now limited and has different rules to eligibility. For example, were Cristiano Ronaldo still playing in 2020, he would be eligible to play for England as he is contracted to Manchester United. So if England were to play Spain now, for instance, we would get to see a forward line up Fernando Torres and Emmanuel Adebayor taking on the likes of Ronaldinho and Lionel Messi. Brazil, meanwhile, will be reduced to minnows of international football in 2020, whilst Scotland have been further depleted following the departure of Celtic and Rangers to England.

So what else can we look forward to in Premier League 2020? Well, there is no need to berate the officials anymore. These have been replaced by Robot Referees, who are programmed with every rule and meet each one to the letter of the law meticulously. So consistently good are these, there is no longer a need for assistant referees as their superfine laser signals can spot an offside decision from up to 100 meters, whilst whenever a ball crosses a line it turns from bright yellow to bright red. These Robot Referees stand at 8 foot tall to avoid intimidation, whilst they hover at a maximum of 80-miles-an-hour so keeping up with play is never a problem.

It is also impossible for matches to be postponed in Premier League 2020, due to the Astroturf surface which is a basic requirement of every club in the top-flight. Not only this, but by the end of the 2023/24 season, it will also be necessary for every stadium to have a retractable roof. Failure to comply with this will likely result in the termination of your Premier League license, which can then only be reapplied for after two years (although this time may be increased for the 'smaller' clubs with lesser global attraction).

As for the players, a maximum wage of £500,000-per-week has now been imposed, and contracts are limited to a maximum of two-years. This allows them to consider moving on a Bosman in twelve months after their first season, whilst it also allows clubs to cash in on them after the same time if it becomes clear the player wants out. And if both player and club are happy, then they can simply settle on a new two-year contract and talk again after another twelve months. Unlike 2008 when players can only appear for a maximum of two clubs each season, players in 2020 can be sold and bought as many times as possible.

As far as the English contingent goes amongst players in Premier League 2020, these are few and far between. A Uefa legislation to introduce six homegrown players in each matchday squad across Europe would, particularly in England, be met with fury and long forgotten as the number of English players plying their trade in their own country continues to dwindle and those who do make it spend much of their time kicking their heels in the reserves or youth teams.

In fact, you would be hard pushed to find English representation anywhere at your club. Every single one of the Premier League clubs will be managed by overseas coaches, who mainly employ their compatriots to their backroom staff. You may get the occasional Englishman on the board of directors, but most clubs are owned by Americans, whilst others have been taken over by Russians, Thais or Icelandic businessmen looking to make a quick dollar, rouble, baht or krona.

Managers have also been given help with their team selections and decisions, thanks to their electronic Premier Zone equipment. This allows each boss to monitor the performances of their players as well as work-rate, stamina, pass completion, key-contributions and even morale. With just the touch of a button during any game, the Premier Zone unit can also recommend which players are likely to offer the least in the remaining stages of the game, making substitute decisions easier.

So, as we look forward to this exciting new era of Premier League football, what's in it for us fans, so often overlooked until our money is wanted? Predictably, ticket prices have hit the roof. An average season ticket in the Premier League now costs £1,500, although you can expect to pay double that for a Big Four club. Matchday tickets range from £60 to £300, but if you can't afford that you can buy a ticket for the 45-minute section, which allows you to watch half of the match at just over half the price. But be warned – once the 45 minutes is up, a dark barrier emerges from the side of the pitch to block your viewing and you have five minutes to leave the stadium (particularly annoying if you are watching the second half of a gripping match and there is time added on).

If you do decide to go ahead and buy a season ticket for your club, the one-time problem of a waiting list is no longer an issue in 2020 due to the lack of fans who can actually afford one. There is, however, a 'reserve' price which must be paid before you can order your ticket. This usually costs half of your season ticket, and it reserves your seat for another season. So, for example, if your season ticket costs £1,500, you can only buy this once you have reserved your seat at £750.

Once inside the stadium we can watch action replays from the monitor placed on the back of the seat in front for a small price of £10. This can also be used to watch highlights of any other game taking place that day, or you can tune into Goal Flash so you can see every goal from around the country (and sometimes globally) seconds after they happen. And if you have an iWatch, you can even download the full ninety minutes from any game direct to your wrist within seconds of the final whistle.

For those fans who don't like to get too involved in the match and prefer to be entertained, there are non-singing sections in every Premier League 2020 stadium. More expensive than a usual match ticket, access to this part of the ground will allow you the luxury of sitting in a cushioned seat whilst waiter service is available at the touch of a button and earplugs are available in the rare event one of your fellow silent supporters gets over-excited by the action on the pitch. And in case the game is a bore, the blow of forking out for a ticket can be softened by the opportunity to read the daily newspapers or the latest club magazines, which are all available upon request.

But for the fans who like to get behind their team at the game, every ground has a singing section which encourages a lively atmosphere. Chants from previous games are played on the PA systems before the game and at half-time to get the fans going, although these are interrupted every three minutes to play an advert. During the game, when your team is on the attack, your seat starts to vibrate to encourage you to get on your feet and cheer the players on.

Refreshments inside each ground are readily available at competitive prices. You can order a pint of lager or any soft drink for just £7, and there are McDonalds and Burger King Outlets at every side of the ground. For those feeling rather plush, prawn sandwiches are a favourite in many Premier League stadiums, whilst champagne quaffing is also recommended in some of the more expensive seating areas. Be warned though, at most venues you will be expected to tip whoever serves you to the tune of 10%.

If you can't get a ticket for the match, then the next best thing would be to access the game of your choice via Sky Sports at a cost of just £20. And if you have a genuine Premier League HD television (starting price £2000), then you can watch the game in 3D at a cost of just £30. Both options are available only with a twelve-month subscription to the Premier League channel, which starts at just £100-per-month. Once you have subscribed to this, you can also watch every little detail of every single game mulled over and analysed by various former players, pundits and experts on the 'Minute-by-Minute Premier League Show'.

Keeping up with the trends in Premier League 2020 is quite a challenge. Forget the days when clubs changed their strips every two years, now they change every season and have at least five versions – home kit, away kit, third kit, FA Cup kit and USCL/League Cup kit. And should your team reach a cup final, you can expect to fork out for a special 'Limited Edition Cup Final' kit.

The 39th Game: Premier League plays at imperialism

You don't have to buy the kits, of course, but for all Season Ticket holders it is compulsory to buy at least two-a-year.

As Sir Alex Ferguson once so memorably put it: "football, eh? Bloody hell..."

Chapter 12: 'Quotes'

By Mark Carlton

As football fans, we know that we hold very little sway in the modern game. Decisions that affect our clubs and our game are dealt with in the upper echelons of the football hierarchy and are almost completely out of our control. We can voice our opinions and ideas, as we have done for the past seven years at Squarefootball, but ultimately the destiny of the game is held in the sweaty palms of the money men. At the very head of the English game is the FA. They have the potential to make or break the Premier league's decision to pursue the 39th game.

So far the FA has shown a unity and concern over the concept.

***

"The FA has listened carefully to the comments made by Fifa president Sepp Blatter regarding the Premier League's proposal for an international round of fixtures (...)This proposal has generated a high level of debate both domestically and with the international football family. While the FA has given full consideration to views expressed by all parties, we must also make our own position on this subject clear. It was also made

clear (in a meeting with FIFA's general secretary, Jerome Valcke) that the FA has some serious reservations about the proposal. We have a responsibility to the whole of English football and we have to consider any wider consequences and implications that this proposal may create."

FA Chief, Brian Barwick

"The FA has worked extremely hard for several years to improve our relationships and standing with Fifa and Uefa, and has largely succeeded. Clearly we do not want this extensive work to be damaged. We also do not want the Premier League's proposal to affect England's 2018 World Cup bid in any way. At this time, due to the FA's strong international relations, we do not believe it has."

FA Chief Brian Barwick

***

The current FA Chairman, Lord Triesman also outlined his initial concern and echoed Brian Barwick's apprehension about international relations.

"Firstly there are serious problems of congestion in the season, I make it very clear that we would want to make sure that all of our own competitions can be played successfully, and that there isn't the usual overstretch that you get at that time of year which can have an impact on the England side.

"Secondly, I think that we have to make sure that our international relationships are in good shape; there are very many reasons for that, and the 2018 World Cup is one of those reasons.

"Third, there is bound to be continuing concern about whether the 39th game would change the symmetry of the competition or would introduce unfairness as it is perceived in the competition."

FA Chairman Lord Triesman

"We haven't got what I would call a sustainable plan in front of us, the whole of the process requires some fresh thinking and some substantive answers to the questions I've posed. If the Premier League have other proposals, I hope they come back with them relatively quickly."

FA Chairman Lord Triesman

"I am determined that our international and domestic relations must be sustained at the highest level, and I will not countenance any damage to those relations."

FA Chairman Lord Triesman

***

At the very route of the issue is Mr Richard Scudamore, the Chief Executive of the Premier League. Since the concept was first revealed, Scudamore has remained bullish in the face of fierce criticism.

The 39th Game: Premier League plays at imperialism

"This is a huge strategic move, the biggest since the league started, It makes the introduction of pay-per-view look pretty small. The clubs are saying that the time has come. If we don't do it, another sport – or another football league – will do it to us. The league cannot stand still. We are either moving forwards or backwards."

Premier League Chief Executive, Richard Scudamore

Under intense pressure and scrutiny, Scudamore vociferously defended his plans as the integrity of the competition was called into question.

"I admit it is a deviation, albeit a minor one, one thirty-ninth, from perfect symmetry but integrity is a different word. There are inherent unfairnesses in our league, like playing a team coming back from a long trip in Europe or with players injured or suspended. But that is not a lack of integrity. These will all be genuine matches in the middle of the season."

Premier League Chief Executive, Richard Scudamore

Scudamore hinted at a certain American business model that he would like to emulate which must have had a bearing on his formulation of the 39th game concept.

"It will make Superbowl Sunday look small time, we have been wrestling with it for some time because, in the last five years and particularly the last 18 months, we have been inundated with

offers. That reached a crescendo when the NFL came to Wembley."

Premier League Chief Executive, Richard Scudamore

However, cracks begin to appear as the FA and FIFA belatedly get involved, eventually leading to a postponement of a meeting with the world governing body.

"Clearly we are not going to take this forward if it doesn't meet with some form of acquiescence from Fifa, certainly the FA and Football League will have to be comfortable with whatever move and direction we take. We have got until January 2009 to shape any proposals, to consult widely and properly, and to see how we manage to move forward with what is now a global sporting phenomenon."

Premier League Chief Executive, Richard Scudamore

***

"Having consulted with Fifa, we have decided to delay our planned visit whilst we conduct further work prior to addressing them and their confederations formally.

"We sincerely believe that the Premier League has much to offer the development of the game internationally, as witnessed by the many federations and leagues that currently seek our involvement and advice.

"There never has been a rush to conclude these matters and we are more than willing to take time to develop our proposals

further before seeking approval, without which it is not our intention to proceed."

A Premier League Statement

***

FIFA also welcomed the postponement of the meeting.

"Fifa have been advised by the English Premier League that the league, accompanied by senior representatives of the English FA, does not seek a meeting with Fifa at this time to discuss the project of a 39th match day to be played abroad.

"Fifa welcome the Premier League's decision and initiative, which re-establishes the positive and constructive relations between the FA, the FA Premier League and world football's governing body."

FIFA Statement

***

In a typically pompous British way, the Premier League believed that the world would embrace the road show with open arms. Fans around the world may well rejoice at the sight of Manchester United running out to a chorus of high pitched screams in Asia, but many countries and continents have met the idea with a lukewarm reception.

The 39th Game: Premier League plays at imperialism

"We said when this issue first arose last week that FFA's (Football Federation Australia) overwhelming priority is to promote the Hyundai A-League and to continue to invest in, and grow, the game in Australia. That remains our view. The bottom line is, FFA rejects the notion of another country playing a round of their domestic competition in Australia and intruding on the development of the Hyundai A-League and the game in Australia."

Football Federation Australia, Frank Lowy

"It is my belief that it is not a good idea to organise domestic leagues in territories other than their own."

Asian Football Confederation President, Mohamed bin Hammam

"We've been reluctant to have official games played in the US, We'll be guided by Fifa on this matter. But if it's not in line with its rules then we won't sanction it."

US Soccer Chief, Sunil Gulati

"Football fans around the world are more sophisticated than they've been before and everyone wants to see the real thing. This is why when the NFL went to London they took the real thing and that is why the Premier League wants to export the real thing. There is a thirst for Premier League games."

MLS Deputy Commissioner Ivan Gazidis

"It sounds problematic. We are, in principle, opposed to having their Premier League games in Japan, as we have to protect our league and clubs."

The 39th Game: Premier League plays at imperialism

Head of the Japanese FA, Junji Ogura

***

It's all very different for the Chief Executives and Chairman of the 20 Premier League clubs. They can see past the £5million each club is set to make and realise the huge revenue available to them by exploiting the world's thirst for Premier League football. Middlesbrough's Chief Executive, Keith Lamb, has been very vocal in his support for the scheme.

> "It's not all about money but it's not far off when you sit where I do. If we can get £5m out of playing in a foreign country it's a big help. I cannot keep going to the chairman with a begging bowl every year.
>
> "I have got to consider anything that will bring more money into the football club to allow us to buy the best players that we can afford and who want to come to Middlesbrough."
>
> Middlesbrough Chief Executive, Keith Lamb

> "I can only find one flaw in it and that is the one that has been described as the 'sporting integrity flaw', I find it odd that you can play 39 games and it might mean that one of those games is against a team you have to play three times.
>
> "That is the only reason I can find for not doing it."
>
> Middlesbrough Chief Executive, Keith Lamb

Reading Chairman John Madejski and Birmingham's David Gold are also in agreement with Keith Lamb and see the benefits of travelling the globe.

"I think it's common sense that teams should do one match abroad every year. I don't have a problem with it at all. The fans are extremely lucky that they see a wonderful array of foreign talent playing here in England."

Reading chairman John Madejski

"I believe Richard Scudamore's proposal for a 39th game is definitely worth considering and think the negativity about it is extraordinary. A lot of people are saying it is all about money and therefore it has got to be wrong, but I'm afraid money is what gets people out of bed every day.

"The plan to play abroad is still a long way off and I realise there is a great reluctance for change, but you have to be careful about making a gut reaction. There is a groundswell demanding we don't tinker with our great game, but you stand still and you go backwards."

Birmingham Chairman, David Gold

Other clubs have been very cagey with their views and held their cards close to their chest. Sunderland and Tottenham Hotspur both believe the avenue should be explored, but wouldn't commit to the idea in its current form.

The 39th Game: Premier League plays at imperialism

"All that was decided that as a major league, it is something that we ought to examine. We do have lots of overseas fans that are unable to come to matches played in the UK so I think it is something that should be explored."

Tottenham chief executive Daniel Levy

"We have only agreed to explore something, nothing more than that. When we find out more I'll be able to tell you if it is a good idea. We really are at step A and not step B or C."

Sunderland chairman Niall Quinn

Rick Parry, Liverpool's Chief Executive, bucked the trend and opposed the Premier League's plans.

"My biggest concern is for the integrity of the game but I think there are also several other concerns.

"Firstly, it could be illogical from the point of view of the fixture calendar with international games, cup competitions and replays to fit in, so to suggest adding another game – with extra travel – is strange. I think the integrity of the competition is a major issue. I simply cannot get my head around the idea of a situation in which you can play the same team three times in one season.

"You also have to bear in mind the popularity of the Premier League abroad. It is so popular because it is the Premier League in England and nowhere else.

"Whichever way I look at it I think it is a step too far."

Liverpool Chief Executive, Rick Parry

The 39th Game: Premier League plays at imperialism

***

There was also a mixed reaction from the men that will guide their teams on foreign soil if the 39th game goes ahead. Understandably Derby County's Paul Jewell wasn't impressed with the idea, but seeing as he might not be part of the 20 elite clubs by the time this comes to fruition, it's not that surprising.

"I just think it's typical of the Premier League. I think fans are getting less and less important in their eyes. If it's just for money purposes then surely there's enough money swimming around in the game at the moment and it just becomes razzamatazz."
Derby County Manager, Paul Jewell

Liverpool's Rafael Benitez also echoed his concerns and is in complete agreement with his Chief Executive.

"I don't like it, I think to play another game in another country is not right for this competition. You must play here in England with the same opportunities for everyone. The seeding idea is the reason I don't like it. It's important to give everyone the same opportunities.

"If it's just about money, you can organise a tournament in Hong Kong with the top four if you want and you'll have the money that you want, but to change the competition in this way is not fair. It's not a good idea and I don't think it's a solution for anyone."
Liverpool manager, Rafael Benitez

Portsmouth's Harry Redknapp can also see Premier League clubs becoming greedy and wanting more games abroad and in doing this, setting a dangerous precedent.

"Clubs could become like the Harlem Globetrotters. It will start with one game and then next year or the year after until eventually I can see us playing quite a few games in different parts of the world."
Portsmouth manager Harry Redknapp

Wigan Athletic, a team that wouldn't greatly benefit from the move has also understandably questioned the proposal.

"It's bad enough with international friendlies, let alone going overseas. I read the other day that games are going out to 22 or 23 countries. It's quite unbelievable, it gets everywhere, so I wouldn't be surprised, although there will be a few irate people. Can you imagine going to Fergie (Sir Alex Ferguson) and telling him 'by the way, you're not playing at home this week, you are playing in Japan'? I'd like to see it!"
Wigan manager Steve Bruce

Whilst Gareth Southgate obviously doesn't sing from the same hymn sheet as his Chief Executive and thinks someone was just pulling his leg when he heard the news

The 39th Game: Premier League plays at imperialism

"Is it April 1? I find it highly unlikely it would happen. I wouldn't think it would be a realistic proposition."

Middlesbrough manager Gareth Southgate

Some managers decided to sit on the fence due to the early, sketchy details regarding the Premier League's travelling circus.

"It is obviously a marketing thing. I would have to have a clearer picture of what is behind this marketing idea - I would have to find out more about it. One extra game of football a year, as long as the calendar can be sorted out, that doesn't seem to be a deal-breaker - but I have no real opinions at the moment on whether it is a good deal or a bad deal."

Fulham boss Roy Hodgson

"What disappoints me is (United chief executive) David Gill phoned me and said 'keep this quiet, we are going to discuss it' and then it's all over the papers this morning. They can't keep their mouth shut down there.

"I think if they are going to do these things, they should have been enquiring and having discussions with managers and players before they come out with all this stuff and make an issue of it."

Manchester United manager Sir Alex Ferguson

Others were more praiseworthy of the idea and could see the wider benefits and forward thinking the Premier League had adopted.

"I'm not against an innovative attitude if it respects the competitive side of our league, if it respects the fans and promotes the quality of our Premier League."

Arsenal boss Arsene Wenger

"I don't necessarily think it is a bad thing. From what I understand, it has been well thought out. The trouble with a lot of people is when something new comes into the arena, they want to find reasons to knock it. I am not against change."

Newcastle manager Kevin Keegan

As time passed and the idea looked like it was running out of steam, Arsene Wenger still came out in support of the concept.

"The idea looks to be dead, maybe because the idea came out in a brutal way and maybe the PR was not done, now it looks to be an idea which is in a very difficult position. I was open-minded but as well I will not cry if it doesn't happen. I just felt there was something to explore there which will now not be done.

"It looks difficult to resurrect now because Uefa, Fifa and The FA have come out against it. It is a big stream to swim against now."

Arsenal Manager, Arsene Wenger

Two ex-international managers also raised concerns about the effect it will have on the game.

The 39th Game: Premier League plays at imperialism

"The Premier League was formed with the support of the Football Association to improve the standard of English football. The original idea was to have 18 clubs. This was increased to 22 before it was reduced to 20.

"Taking the game abroad is therefore not a move to help the English side.

"With so many foreign players in the Premier League it is always going to be a difficult job for England to make their mark. If the Premier League continues to go in the direction it is at the moment the more difficult it will become."

Former England Manager, Graham Taylor

"Other national associations won't be happy about the Premier League coming into their game, taking sponsors, taking advertising, taking revenue from their game."

Former Northern Ireland and Fulham manager, Lawrie Sanchez

***

As well has raising issues that would affect the game in general, the PFA and Football Supporter's Federation obviously had concerns for the welfare of players and supporters.

"The Premier League is the biggest, strongest league in the world and the most financially successful but that doesn't mean it always sits cosily with other interests and one of those interests is the England international team.

The 39th Game: Premier League plays at imperialism

"What is becoming paramount is the need for a midwinter break but instead of that, the gap is going to be used to extend the demands on players."

Professional Footballers' Association chief executive Gordon Taylor

"I challenge the Premier League to abandon this proposal if it turns out that the majority of supporters are opposed to it and that would be my confident prediction.

"This game relies on having supporters in the ground and when the day comes that they completely think that match-going fans are of no value, then that's the day when the game will severely suffer."

Malcolm Clarke, co-chairman of the Football Supporters' Federation

***

The subject evoked so many different opinions, even the government decided to voice their opinion.

"English football is hugely popular around the world and I understand the Premier League's desire to take the game to new audiences but this proposal goes beyond the Premier League and careful consideration is needed before any decisions are made... Money and merchandising must not take priority over the interests of fans in this country. The Premier League brings great benefits to Britain, but it's success today is established upon local club

support built up over generations. The game must never forget its roots."

Secretary of State for Culture, Media and Sport, Andy Burnham

"Let's see what the fans say about this. I think it's important to recognise that all the money has got to go back into the game, so that the fans get the benefit."

Prime Minister, Gordon Brown

All these opinions boil down to nothing if these next quotes have any gravitas, and they do because they are from the head men at FIFA and UEFA.

***

"The Premier League is richer than the others, they have more responsibility and what they are trying to do is contrary to this responsibility. This is something I cannot understand and definitely the Fifa executive committee will not sanction such an initiative."

FIFA President, Sepp Blatter

"It's a strange and comical idea, I was laughing. I laughed because it will never be received by Fifa, by the fans and by the national associations. It's a nonsense idea. It's like if I am president of Uefa and I put the house of Uefa in China.

"It's ironic. Soon you will have in England no English presidents, you already have no English coach, you have no

English players and maybe now you will have no clubs playing in England. It's a joke."

UEFA President, Michel Platini

"I am sorry, but the business of China needs to belong to the clubs of China, but [the Premier League] want to expand their sponsors, their TV rights. It's always for the same reason.

"You should always represent your fans. I don't know why you have to play in China, because your fans are in Liverpool or in Wigan or Portsmouth. If you belong to a team, you play for your team and your city.

"I had a phone call with Mr Blatter this morning and we share the same idea that it's the responsibility of the national associations, and I am sure they will never accept it because it's not good for football. I think the FA of England will oppose it. The beauty of football is you have some values, you have the teams, you have the fans, you represent something important and you are not a travelling circus. You are not a show, we are part of 100 years of history."

UEFA President, Michel Platini

Chapter 13: Was it worth it?

By Antony Melvin

"I am amazed, yet actually not particularly surprised by the suggestion. I don't really know whether I should be appalled or whether I should laugh about it. It definitely does not fit in with the notion of Corporate Social Responsibility which was adopted at the 2007 FIFA Congress. Everyone needs to assume their own responsibilities. Those who think that they are the best - i.e. the Premier League - should first and foremost demonstrate their social responsibility to others.

"If you oppose the FIFA World Cup decision-makers - namely the FIFA Executive Committee - then you cannot expect the very same board to make a decision in your favour. But I do not want to rule out the chances of any country that wishes to host the 2018 FIFA World Cup."

Sepp Blatter, February 2008

It took eight weeks after the news broke about the International Round' before the fuss over the proposal finally started to subside.

Sepp Blatter, who seems more and more interested in the English game with every passing newsflash, is clearly dead set against the idea. On 14 March Blatter took time out from a meeting about a corruption allegation to reiterate his desire to avoid international club football for the Premier League, a stance that has the full backing of his committee:

"This idea for the Premier League to play a 39th round outside country does not work. They would be playing 12 hours away west and east and 24 hours difference in the south. Even the former chairman of the FA, Mr Geoff Thompson, said we should oppose it."

But to date the Premier League remain committed to the plan, even if there is now talk of a 'one year consultation' over the proposals.

The FIFA organisation does have a big stick to wield in awarding (or indeed not awarding) the 2018 World Cup to England. After a gap of over 50 years the country that took football to the world is certainly due a turn at hosting the biggest football event around. The prospect of damaging the chances of an English bid was, reportedly, the cause of much friction between the Premier League, as embodied by Richard Scudamore and the FA in the form of Lord Triesman.

The very fact that the top clubs in England have their own governing body and agenda somewhat separate from the national team and the majority of English football means that the clubs can ignore the needs of the national team - or the country at large.

Although if the calculations suggested that the international round would generate less money for the clubs than hosting the World Cup then that would represent a bitter irony if England lost the 2018 tournament as a result.

But the FA are on shaky ground if they merely oppose the international round on the basis of greed; given that the cost of Wembley has included the removal of the popular 'England on the road' fixtures and the removal of FA Cup semi-finals from club grounds as well as delaying the Burton-on-Trent project.

With such widespread opposition to the proposal, from fans groups to the leading football politicians there seems to be little chance that it will be allowed to happen. The only likely scenario would now involve a country that has little to fear from a FIFA reprimand, say Qatar, agreeing to take the whole package.

But regardless of the bullish comments from Scudamore on 20 February 2008:

"It has only just started and we have only had 10 days of a year-long consultation process. This is a set of proposals which is a work in progress and yes, it has had some hostile reaction ... but it's still in its infancy."

... the most likely scenario is that the Premier League will quietly drop the plan, and announce some different idea during the dead zone in England when Euro 2008 is taking place.

If the Premier League continue to press forward there is the prospect of irrevocable damage to the World Cup bid taking place;

and that might not be acceptable to a number of people who could undermine Richard Scudamore.

The idea that the Premier League is able to openly discuss games beyond national boundaries does raise the spectre of a European Super League or another competition that will amputate much of English football from the elite. But perhaps that is a fight for another time.

***

The final act of the Premier League season 2007/8 saw both Chelsea and Manchester United battle out the final day separated by goal difference. The same four sides, as ever, filled the top four places. And English football's dominance of the agenda was confirmed when the latter stages of the Champions' League was once again dominated by English clubs; with an all-English final the result. This is not the 39th game, but in many ways it could be the precursor.

The Premier League has fended off the very idea that this oligopoly is 'boring' and Richard Scudamore was still adamant as late as 11 May that the 'international round' was viable for all clubs, not merely the 'big four'. Far from being quietly abandoned, perhaps the FA will try to seize some support by embracing a broader church during the summer months:

"The Premier League are [sic] a unique proposition. Our strength is the aggregate of all our clubs, but it would be wrong to assume that there is no interest in the clubs outside the top four.

The 39th Game: Premier League plays at imperialism

"It is a natural progression to take all our teams around the world. There is no doubt that there is scope to increase interest levels around the world.

"We need to find the right vehicle and format - and that is still in the melting pot."

For now the Premier League rages against the dying light of its 'International Round' proposal. Perhaps in five years time football will look back and wonder what all the fuss was about – but equally the Premier League could have won the argument that many people assume is already lost. Stranger things have happened.

References

Chapter 1: 'Premier League mulls overseas games'

http://football.uk.reuters.com/premiership/news/L07742906.php

http://football.guardian.co.uk/comment/story/0,9753,1606114,00.html

http://www.rte.ie/sport/2000/0412/keaneroy.html

http://football.guardian.co.uk/Columnists/Column/0,,1871941,00.html

Chapter 2: Premier League 1992 - 2008

http://www.deloitte.com/dtt/press_release/0,1014,sid%253D2834%2526cid%253D159168,00.html

http://www.premierleague.com/page/History/0,,12306,00.html

http://www.football-league.premiumtv.co.uk/page/History/0,,10794,00.html

http://en.wikipedia.org/wiki/Premier_League

http://www.le.ac.uk/sociology/css/resources/factsheets/fs8.html

The Daily Telegraph Chronicle of Football by Norman Barrett

http://www.brainyquote.com/quotes/authors/s/sepp_blatter.html

Chapter 3: The 39th step could be a good thing

http://en.wikipedia.org/wiki/Premier_League

http://www.rsssf.com

http://www.arsenal.com/article.asp?thisNav=news&article=487357&lid=NewsHeadline&Title=Wenger+-+We+could+play+abroad+but+not+just+for+money
http://en.wikipedia.org/wiki/Parkinson's_law

http://www.telegraph.co.uk/sport/main.jhtml?xml=/sport/2008/02/15/sfnfro415.xml&page=1

http://news.bbc.co.uk/sport1/hi/football/eng_prem/7254893.stm

http://www.skysports.com/story/0,19528,11095_3183764,00.html

Chapter 4: The 39th game would be a bad move

The 39th Game: Premier League plays at imperialism

http://www.bbc.co.uk/sport1/hi/football/eng_prem/7243949.stm

http://www.bbc.co.uk/sport1/hi/football/eng_prem/7239788.stm

http://www.bbc.co.uk/sport1/hi/football/eng_prem/7232856.stm

http://www.bbc.co.uk/sport1/hi/football/eng_prem/7232856.stm

Chapter 5: The 39th game has logic

None

Chapter 6/7: Eating at the top table and waiting on

http://www.brainyquote.com/quotes/quotes/j/johnmilton391641.html

http://www.brainyquote.com/quotes/quotes/j/johnmilton122739.html

Arsenal: http://www.timesonline.co.uk/tol/sport/football/premier_league/article3330734.ece

Blackburn Rovers: http://www.bbc.co.uk/dna/606/A32186603

Chelsea: http://www.CFC.net

http://www.timesonline.co.uk/tol/sport/football/premier_league/article3330734.ece

Everton:

Fulham: http://www.fulhamfc.com/Club/Messageboard.aspx?mode=thread&TopicID=36749&page=2

Liverpool: http://www.timesonline.co.uk/tol/sport/football/premier_league/article3330734.ece

Manchester United: http://manchesterunited.rivals.net

Newcastle United: http://www.toonarmyusa.com

Tottenham Hotspur: http://beefbagel.com/bagel/2008/02/the-39th-step-a-step-too-far/; http://www.bbc.co.uk/dna/606/A32152367

http://www.timesonline.co.uk/tol/sport/football/premier_league/article3330734.ece

West Ham United: http://ww.ozhammers.com

Wigan Athletic:

http://boards.footymad.net/mboard/fmb.php?tno=558&fid=516&sty=2&act=1&mid=2130602613

http://boards.footymad.net/mboard/fmb.php?tno=558&fid=516&sty=2&act=1&mid=2130602613

Chapter 8: From European League To World League?

The 39th Game: Premier League plays at imperialism

None

Chapter 9: What about the rest of us?

http://www.afcwimbledon.co.uk/aboutthetrust.php?Psub_nav_id=2&Psection_id=10&Psub_section_id=63

Chapter 10: The Greed League

http://en.wikipedia.org/wiki/Michael_Knighton

http://en.wikipedia.org/wiki/Gordon_Gekko

Chapter 11: Premier League 2020

The Observer, September 30 2007

http://en.wikipedia.org/wiki/The_Football_League#History

Chapter 12: Quotes

http://football.guardian.co.uk/News_Story/0,,2257261,00.html

http://www.timesonline.co.uk/tol/sport/football/article3330640.ece

http://www.footballfanscensus.com/surveys/arguments.html?survey_id=338

http://news.bbc.co.uk/sport1/hi/football/eng_prem/7254528.stm

http://www.telegraph.co.uk/sport/main.jhtml?xml=/sport/2008/02/09/sfnbon109.xml

http://www.skysports.com/story/0,19528,11095_3183764,00.html

http://itn.co.uk/news/b007086ce3fdd8bf907f6c0efaea8133.html

http://www.mirror.co.uk/sport/football/2008/02/22/39th-game-plan-is-football-s-version-of-ann-summers-says-birmingham-supremo-david-gold-89520-20327557/

http://www.dailymail.co.uk/pages/live/articles/sport/football.html?in_article_id=514125&in_page_id=1779

http://www.dailymail.co.uk/pages/live/articles/sport/football.html?in_article_id=513903&in_page_id=1779

http://www.dailymail.co.uk/pages/live/articles/sport/football.html?in_article_id=514111&in_page_id=1779

http://www.timesonline.co.uk/tol/sport/football/premier_league/liverpool/article3372040.ece

http://www.liverpooldailypost.co.uk/liverpool-fc/liverpool-fc-news/2008/02/16/rick-parry-39th-game-is-a-step-too-far-64375-20484339/

The 39th Game: Premier League plays at imperialism

http://news.bbc.co.uk/sport1/hi/football/teams/m/middlesbrough/7230549.stm

http://news.bbc.co.uk/sport1/hi/football/eng_prem/7239788.stm

http://news.bbc.co.uk/sport1/hi/football/teams/d/derby_county/7246612.stm

http://news.bbc.co.uk/sport1/hi/football/eng_prem/7232856.stm

Chapter 13: Was it worth it?

http://ukpress.google.com/article/ALeqM5ifDCi5ERA15gW0sZj3btrz-7qtQA

http://www.fifa.com/aboutfifa/federation/president/news/newsid=691919.html

http://football.guardian.co.uk/News_Story/0,,2259092,00.html

http://www.guardian.co.uk/football/2008/feb/20/newsstory.premierleague

http://www.skysports.com/story/0,19528,11661_3545957,00.html

www.ingramcontent.com/pod-product-compliance
Lightning Source LLC
Chambersburg PA
CBHW022104160426
43198CB00008B/349